Raising Charitable Children

When you are finished with this book, please:

Pass it along to the next reader

or

Return to the AACPS Department of Partnerships, Development & Marketing
2644 Riva Rd, Annapolis.

Raising Charitable Children

Carol Weisman

MSW, CSP, MOM

PRESIDENT, BOARD BUILDERS, INC.

Raising Charitable Children

By Carol Weisman, MSW, CSP, MOM

Published by F.E. Robbins & Sons Press
St. Louis, Missouri

Copyright 2006 by F.E. Robbins & Sons Press. Revised 2008.
8025 Maryland, Suite 5A
St. Louis, MO 63105
314-863-4422
www.raisingcharitablechildren.com

Cover and text layout by
Riezebos Holzbaur Design Group, San Francisco, CA

Printed in the United States of America. Third printing.

ISBN-10: 0-9767972-0-8
ISBN-13: 978-09767972-0-3

This book is
dedicated to my mother,
Renate Dohrn-Weisman, M.D.,
who gave both money and
fabulous advice with no strings
attached—and who also knew
when to keep both her mouth
and her pocketbook shut!

Contents

Raising Charitable Children

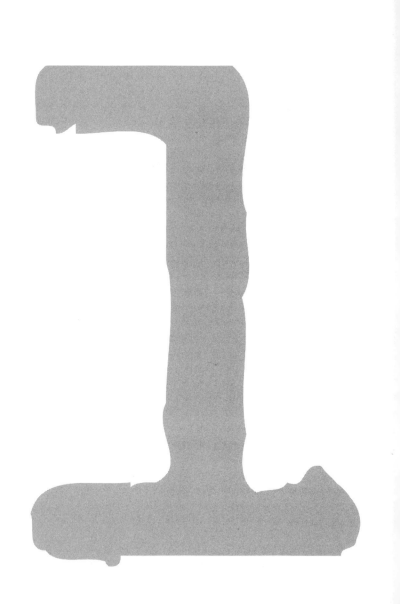

Introduction
Getting Past Gimme-Gimme

When I heard my youngest son say his first word—"Donalds," short for McDonald's—I knew I was in trouble. When he was two, he told me he wanted a Walker mobile home and a Remington electric shaver for Christmas. He could barely walk, yet already Jono was latching onto the consumerist, "gimme-gimme" mindset that permeates our society. I could see that some major values education was needed—otherwise, my angelic, golden-haired child was going to turn into a materialistic, selfish little brat.

My husband was stationed at Fort Bragg, North Carolina, back then (this was in the early 1980s), and we weren't going to be able to see family that Christmas. To ease my homesickness, I baked cookies with my boys, then ages two and three-and-a-half, and made a heartening discovery: When we took the cookies over to the Army hospital, my little consumers gleefully forgot about themselves and happily handed out their tasty gifts to the patients.

The experience reminded me of an important lesson. It put a halt to the little pity party I was throwing myself. So I wasn't going home for the holidays—but unlike the young men in the hospital, I wouldn't be spending Christmas staring at gray walls and an IV line, either. I would have my sons, my husband and a tree.

Turned out I wasn't the only one who learned something valuable that day. On the way home, my son Teddy said, "Sometimes the cookies you give away taste the best."

It was then that I realized an even bigger moral to the story—it doesn't take much to show kids how great giving can feel.

Today, as a professional speaker on philanthropy, governance, volunteerism and fundraising, I give countless keynote addresses at nonprofit conferences, benefits and banquets. Almost always, when someone is honored for a donation or grant, he or she says, "I'm the one who has benefited the most from this gift." In fact, Charles Ackerman—the T-shirt king of Sarasota, Florida, and a major donor to Jewish Family and Children's Service of Sarasota-Manatee—once used those exact words at a small, private dinner I attended with him to discuss the dedication of a building that would be named in his honor. The very next week, I saw a former welfare mother, who was also an incest survivor and recovering crack addict, tell the audience at another nonprofit's annual meeting, "In volunteering, for the first time I got more than I gave. Sharing my story with your youth group and listening to their stories has been the high point of my life, and I thought I knew what 'high' was all about." I was stunned by how similarly she and Charles Ackerman spoke, even though their life experiences couldn't have been more different.

Children today are inundated with all kinds of messages about being consumers—to want for themselves rather than to give of themselves. But putting a cell phone in their pockets and the right shoes on their feet will never provide the long-term happiness fix children crave. What they need even more is the warmth of human contact—the warmth that comes from giving more than receiving.

I, for one, believe that such fulfillment is quite infectious. Whenever I mention the titles of other books I've written on non-profit management—*Losing Your Executive Director without Losing Your Way; Build a Better Board in 30 Days: A Practical Guide for Busy Trustees*—people's eyes glaze over. Whenever I mention this book, eyes light up, and people ask me how they can be guaranteed a copy.

Americans are stunningly generous. We give time. We give money. According to the Giving USA Foundation, charitable donations made by both individuals and private organizations in 2004 totaled a whopping $248.52 billion dollars—a five percent increase from the previous year and an all-time record high.

Of course, Americans by no means own the market on charitable gifts and actions. In the United Kingdom, a non-profit group called the Citizenship Foundation acts as a liaison between charities and government to nurture a nationwide culture of giving. Part of the foundation's work is the teen-oriented group G-Nation, which offers school curricula on philanthropy and sponsors an annual, week-long, nationwide celebration of kids making a differ-ence in the world. In Australia—a country in which, unlike the U.S., there's an overwhelming belief that it's the govern-ment's job to provide wherever there is need—there was an estimated jump in volunteerism of 192 million work hours between 1995 and 2000, while tax-deductible donations increased from approximately $632 million to $702.5 million between the 1998–1999 and 1999–2000 fiscal years. The Canadian non-profit clearinghouse Imagine Canada estimates that volunteering and donating in Canada adds $75.9 billion annually to its national economy.

In recent years, the world's desire to do good by others has been strongly tested. The terrorist attacks of 9/11, the tsunami in Asia and Hurricane Katrina have each challenged us as individuals to recognize the needs of others, no matter who they are or where they live, and to reach out when help is needed. The global population has responded time and again with ferocious generosity. In the month after Hurricane Katrina hit, the Red Cross received $946.6 million in gifts and pledges from around the world. After the tragedy of 9/11, the September 11th Fund was established to help those affected through cash assistance, employment assistance, health care, mental counseling and legal aid. Its celebrity-studded telethon brought in $129,076,000; overall, the fund received $399,379,000 and carried out its duties so well and so efficiently that it disbanded three years later having met its goals. Heck, Sandra Bullock even donated $1 million of her own money to the Red Cross for tsunami relief—more than The Gap, Lockheed Martin, Whole Foods, Tiffany's, and Sprint combined! This is consistent with donation trends in the U.S.—it is individuals, not corporations, who do the bulk of the financial giving. (According to the Giving USA Foundation's 2004 findings, 75.6 percent of total giving in America comes from individuals; only 4.8 percent comes from corporations.)

14

This is an astounding legacy of philanthropy that we have all created—one we need to pass on to the next and future generations. Volunteerism and charity work are rife with meaningful, memorable, win-win experiences—plus, a lot of the time, they're just plain fun.

Last year, while I was sitting in my friend Michelle Kornberg's kitchen in Melbourne, Australia—which really is one of the best places on earth to visit—she told me about something her 15-year-old son Daniel had recently done. I'll always remember the look of pride on her face when she recounted how Daniel and two of his buddies had saved up their money for a charity auction benefiting the hospital where Daniel's father worked. Display tables were set out with all kinds of luxurious, snazzy items up for bid: trips, autographed athletic memorabilia, etc. But Daniel and his friends bypassed all that and went to a table showcasing, of all things, medical supplies. Actually, they were just photos of medical supplies, mostly high-tech, huge pieces of equipment the hospital needed. Daniel and his friends placed the highest bid of the night on a high-end electrothermometer. They were thrilled to donate such a cool piece of equipment to the hospital and only wished it could have been something larger and more elaborate. I can just imagine these boys getting together year after year to buy more and more significant gifts for the hospital, enjoying every minute of it.

When I started to write this book, dozens and dozens of people called or e-mailed me to tell me stories like this—charitable deeds their kids had done, or their neighbor's kids had done, or their sister's kids or their parish's kids or their local preschool's kids. As I started collecting all these stories, I also started to wonder: How did these kids manage to pull off these acts of charity and volunteerism? Certainly the seven-year-old didn't drive the truck of donated canned goods to the soup kitchen himself. Surely the nine-year-old who wanted to start her own foundation did not singlehandedly apply for 501(c)3 status from the Secretary of State. How did they get to this place, and what did the adults in their lives do to make it happen?

I realized that it's the parents and other caring adults that facilitate a lot of this do-gooding, and so I decided to write *Raising Charitable Children* as a how-to guide for them. Each chapter in this book begins with a true (and quite inspiring, I must say) story of a child or group of children who have made a difference in the world, big or small. (And speaking of small, do remember that small is not a bad way to help. Not every child is supposed to raise a million dollars or head up his or her own non-profit board of directors.) These stories address many of the Big Questions, indicated at the start of each chapter, about introducing charity and philanthropy to kids of all ages, abilities and backgrounds. The how-to questions that follow break down these projects into manageable steps for the adults in charge.

Such endeavors will always need to be approached with caution and respect, and so I do have a few words of warning. Some people volunteer because they want what I call "emotional access to the frontlines." They believe they can help others by sharing in their emotional burdens, by being front-and-center with them when tragedy or adversity unfolds. You really have to be careful with this. Charity isn't about voyeurism. When I worked as a medical social worker in a pediatric hospital, I came across many,

many volunteers who wanted to talk to the children with cancer and their families. They really wanted to help, but also, they wanted to be part of the experience. Families fighting a foe like cancer, though, deserve their privacy. The same is true with the beneficiaries of your work. They deserve their privacy, and it's important to teach this respect to children.

As you approach volunteerism, keep in mind the humanity of those you are attempting to help. Sometimes your work will be best done from afar. When introducing philanthropy into a child's life, demonstrate that there are many, many ways to help, and that while not all volunteer and charity opportunities can prove thrilling or visceral, all are necessary, even when carried out from a distance.

To respect the privacy of some of the individuals whose stories I've shared in this book, I've referred to them by a changed first name only. Where I've referred to somebody by a first and last name, the name is real.

When researching and trying out new charitable opportunities, always remember that the relationship has to work for all the parties involved. That means you, the other grown-ups, the kids, and the organization. Some nonprofits simply may not be established enough, or have their act together enough, to handle you and your fellow volunteers. They may not have the physical space for you to work on-site, or their staff won't know what to do with you, or there aren't enough staff members to work with you. Such shortcomings are more common than you might think. A charity has never turned down my money, but more than a few have turned down gifts of my time and expertise.

As you begin your family's journey into charity and philanthropy, it can be tricky to predict how much responsibility will fall on you and how much will fall on your child (or grandchild, godchild, etc.). We've all eaten far too many Girl Scout cookies that have never been touched by a child's hand, but rather sold to us through a co-worker whose daughter just happens to be a Girl Scout. But since kids don't drive, schedule their own agendas or enjoy secretarial support at the office, their projects often wind up becoming our projects. It's like getting a puppy: Despite a child's passionate promises to take full responsibility for Scruffy, Mom and Dad still find themselves scooping poop off the neighbor's lawn at one o'clock in the morning—not necessarily because the child is shirking his or her duties, but because the doggie's gotta go, and the kid's already in bed.

Sharing the load without owning your child's project can prove to be one of the trickiest parts of taking on volunteer work. You have to be truly honest about what the child is mature enough to handle and what you have the time to commit to. If you ever reach a point where it feels like your kid is taking credit for the work you're doing, then something is off-balance! Your role is to do the adult things that your children need you to do so that they can pursue the charitable goals they've set for themselves, or that you've collectively set together. This means you chaperone, supervise, and do a little literal and figurative heavy lifting.

Lastly, don't get discouraged. Sometimes kids would rather play video games than stack cans in a food pantry— just as there are days when I'd rather watch reruns of *Everybody Loves Raymond* than go to another board meeting. This is where you have to be both wise and tenacious. It can be really frustrating to work with a charity or a child who

18

isn't into what you have to offer. Don't get discouraged. It may take some time to find a philanthropic project that's a good fit, but once you do, trust me—you and your kids will feel great about it.

Give 'til It Feels Good

The Big Question: How can I start teaching my kids about the joys of giving when they're still very young?

When our sons turned five and six, my husband and I decided to start a new family tradition. On their birthdays, each child would get to make a small financial donation to the charity of his choice. The donations were not in lieu of a party or gifts, but in addition to them. At such a young age, giving should be a totally joyful experience, so we didn't want to make them forsake some of their birthday fun in the name of charity. If a child thinks that every time he gives, he loses something, then the joy of giving is diminished.

We talked to our sons about the things they enjoyed and why. Jono, our five-year-old, wanted to give a gift to the Missouri Botanical Garden, a place our family often visited on weekends. His logic was sound: He loved the toasted cheese sandwiches at their café. Teddy planned on becoming a scientist and a break dancer. When he found out that the non-profit arts group Dance St. Louis didn't offer break-dance performances, he chose to give his donation to the St. Louis Science Center instead.

I called the development directors at both places and told them that I would like to come by with the kids to make a modest contribution. (Note: "Development director" is non-profit code for "fundraiser.") When we brought Teddy to deliver his gift, the staff at the Science Center couldn't have been nicer. They gave him a wonderful behind-the-scenes tour, even though they were only receiving a small donation on his behalf.

At the Botanical Garden, the development director, a very stylish woman named Pat Rich, asked if she might contact the press about Jono's donation. I said that would be fine. She called again and asked if we could meet with Dr. Peter Raven, the Garden's director. Jono decided to bring an extra gift for Dr. Raven—a pair of Groucho Marx glasses, complete with fake nose and moustache, left over from his birthday party. The Botanical Garden staff gave Jono a T-shirt and a Frisbee filled with fish food (to feed to the koi in the Garden's pond), then took a picture of him and Dr. Raven in the rose garden, wearing their Groucho Marx glasses and shaking hands. We still have a copy of that photo hanging in our family room.

Two weeks later, we went back to the Botanical Garden for one of our usual weekend visits. Jono was snooping around like a little bloodhound. When I asked him what he was looking for, he said that he wanted to find the plaque with his name on it. I explained that he was going to have to give a whole lot more than twenty bucks to get his own plaque!

My sons are men now, but my husband and I still make yearly birthday donations in their names. When Jono went to Alfred University in upstate New York to earn his B.F.A. in ceramics, he decided that, even as a student, he'd give his birthday donation to his future alma mater. Jono's love of clay-making began at age five, when he started taking classes at a local art studio called Craft Alliance—a non-profit co-op that wound up receiving Jono's birthday donation the year he turned six.

"I remember thinking that, because of my gift, they wouldn't ever run out of clay," Jono recalls. And while he never got his name on a plaque at the Missouri Botanical Garden, he did get to carve it into a brick that was laid into the sidewalk outside Craft Alliance, alongside the names of other donors.

Jono is now an art teacher at McClure North High School outside St. Louis. All these years later, he takes his own art students on field trips to visit Craft Alliance, where he always shows them his namesake brick—a real bargain at only $20!

When Teddy went to New York University, he fell in love with the Metropolitan Museum of Art, which received his donation during his freshman year. Teddy still lives in New York City, working as an actor and activist, and he puts a lot of thought into his birthday donations. Nowadays he's more likely to contribute to smaller, grassroots organizations—like El Puente, a tiny community center he came across in his Brooklyn neighborhood. Says Teddy, "There are people who are going to leave millions to the Met, but nobody is going to die and leave a fortune to El Puente."

The important thing for me is that my sons have grown up to consider themselves philanthropists. Not only do they believe that they have something to offer others in terms of time and money—they also believe that such giving is their responsibility and a privilege.

How-To Questions

At what age should I introduce my child to charitable giving?

I would recommend beginning charitable giving at three or four years old. Even at that young age, children understand giving and caring. You see it when toddlers are playing; if one of them gets hurt or starts crying, the other will often put down his or her toy to come over and offer solace.

Most children also possess enough verbal skills by that age to discuss what they enjoy, what they care about, and how they want to help others. Some children, however, may be slow talkers, and you may need to wait an extra year or two to start discussing birthday donations with them.

How do I help my child decide where to donate?

Ask your child a simple question like, "What did you enjoy doing this past year?" Or, "What makes you happy?" No matter what the answer, you can help your child make a relevant donation, demonstrating how he or she can spread joy and happiness to others. Even if your child says something as simple as "I like to watch TV," you can point out that popular kids' programs like *Sesame Street* rely on donations from people just like him or her to stay on the air.

We once told some friends about our birthday tradition, and they decided to try it with their son, Ethan. When they asked him what made him happy that year—a year when they moved cross-country, leaving behind his school, friends and grandparents—Ethan replied that his stuffed animals had helped, because "they make me feel safe when I am scared." His parents asked, "Would you like to pick out a stuffed animal to help another child feel safe?" He said yes, and they took him to buy a stuffed lion. Then, at the suggestion of their church pastor, he gave the lion away at a local food pantry where children would often go with their parents to pick up food for the family. Ethan gave very clear instructions to the food pantry director: "Tell the little boy that when he is afraid, he doesn't even need to talk out loud. He can think brave thoughts and the lion will help him." Ethan left feeling powerful and happy.

How should I contact the charity about my child's donation?

Although the Internet provides endless opportunities to research organizations and make donations online, I don't suggest this as a first means of contact, especially if it's a local charity. Instead, call the group's development office (the fundraising arm of an organization) and ask if you can bring your child to make the donation in person. Explain that this is your child's birthday gift to others, and that this is one way you are teaching your child about charity and philanthropy. I bet you'll find that the staff couldn't be happier to accommodate you and to help make the occasion memorable and special.

How much money should we give?

It depends on your resources, of course. In my family, we started with a token amount, about $20, and increased it over the years as our ability to give increased. You might decide to donate a percentage of the cost of your child's birthday party. So if you spent, say, $50 on the cake, hats

25

and favors, you'll donate half of that, or $25, to your child's charity. But the bottom line is, the amount doesn't matter. It's about teaching your child to think about others on an occasion that's usually all about eating cake and getting toys.

Can we give something other than money?

Yes—in fact, looking back, I wish we had helped our sons do more than just hand over a check to a charity. A child's time is a wonderful donation. One year, my best friend and our combined three kids made sandwiches to give away at a shelter for her son's birthday, because he had recently watched a news program on homelessness. We called a local shelter and asked what kind of food they needed and how they would like it to be packaged. Then we made 100 sandwiches (which took much less time than you'd think), packed them up and dropped them off. The experience had an added bonus—it prompted a very meaningful discussion with our children about the challenges of living on the street.

Should my child become more involved as he or she grows older?

Absolutely. For very little children, putting the stamp on the envelope and dropping it in the mailbox is a great amount of participation. Children old enough to use the phone and the Internet should be encouraged to research charities on their own and choose one that's a good fit.

What if I don't approve of my child's choice of charity?

As children get older, deciding where to contribute and why can become a very personal matter for them—which can get a little hairy, should their beliefs not fall in line with yours. If you don't share your child's opinion, you don't have to put your money where his or her mouth is—but you do have to have the conversation exploring your different sets of values. In other words, you can say no, but not without an explanation.

I do this all the time in my work as a non-profit consultant. There are charities I respect but do not believe in. If these groups ever call asking me to work with them, I respectfully decline and refer them to another consultant. I don't think these people are bad or crazy. They're honest people of good faith, but I just don't happen to share their opinion.

Ultimately, there may be times when you and your child have to agree to disagree, or make small compromises. For example, let's say your child wants to donate to an animal shelter that doesn't have a "no-kill" policy. You may personally oppose these kinds of shelters, but maybe it's the only shelter within a large radius that still does lots of good for stray animals. In a case such as this, you may want to relax your stance for the greater good.

How can we preserve our birthday-donation memories?

In carrying out our birthday tradition, this was the biggest mistake I made. With nothing down on paper, my family just can't remember the details of which child gave to which charity on which birthday, and why. At the very least, write down the charities to which your children donate each year. If you are blessed with the craft gene, keep a scrapbook. If you are a techie, home video is a great way to remember. I would love to have an interview with Teddy on tape, talking about why he wanted to become a break-dancer, or Jono discussing the Missouri Botanical Garden's delicious toasted cheese sandwiches.

27

The Joy and Sadness Meeting

The Big Question: How can I make charity and philanthropy a fun and rewarding family tradition?

A friend of mine once introduced me to a very wealthy businessman who wanted my help setting up a charitable foundation in his family's name. Thomas could do almost anything. He could make millions of dollars, he could attract beautiful women. The one thing Thomas couldn't do was talk to his three sons from his three failed marriages.

Thomas thought he'd invite some of the "boys" from his corporate board of directors to serve on the foundation's board. I asked, "If it's a family foundation, why not invite your kids?" At my suggestion, this titan of industry turned pale and shrank at least two inches. He was reluctant—his youngest son was only five years old, his 21-year-old son had Down syndrome, and he and his 26-year-old son barely spoke. I assured him that each son would be mature enough to handle the discussion. Despite Thomas' misgivings, he agreed.

When we met, everybody was edgy. This was the first time the four of them had ever sat in a room together without the mothers/ex-wives present. I told them that the purpose of the meeting was to figure out the family foundation's priorities.

I began the meeting with this question: "In the last year, what made you happy?" The five-year-old was the first to respond. He said that Chester, his new puppy, made him happy. When I asked why, he said, "Chester is smart and funny, and when I come home, he is always there for me."

The oldest son, an aspiring actor, said, "I saw a play that I couldn't stop thinking about. It made me realize that people don't live forever, and that you can't hate forever. It's the reason I'm here today."

There was stunned silence. Thomas said, "I'm glad you saw that play."

The son with Down syndrome said, "I love my softball team. I like to run and slide into the plate. I even like the smell of the dirt."

Finally, I turned to Thomas and asked him, "What made you happy?" He puffed up his chest, sat up straight and said, "Last year I scored a hole-in-one." I asked him why that was so special. He looked at me like I was a total moron.

I rephrased my question. "Please explain to your sons why, for a man as accomplished as you, a hole-in-one was such a major event."

He said, "I was with three friends, and they were both happy for me and jealous of me. We had a big celebration at the clubhouse and everyone knew about my hole-in-one."

I then asked what made each of them want to cry in the last year. Once again, the five-year-old wanted to start.

He said, "Chester makes me very sad." The oldest son asked why. The five-year-old replied, "Something could happen to Chester and he wouldn't be waiting for me when I come home."

The son with Down syndrome said, "I hate diabetes and having to stick needles in myself."

The oldest son said, "I hate sitting by the phone after auditioning for a play, waiting and waiting and waiting. I eat ice cream all day, and then I feel sick and fat and miserable."

Thomas said proudly, "Nothing makes me cry."

I tried a different approach. "Could you instead talk about a time in your life when you felt sad?"

He thought for a few moments and then said, "I watched my mother die, day by day, of cancer. Every day, there was less of her and more of the cancer. By the end, she was drugged all the time. I hated the way the hospital smelled. I hated the nurses for not coming in more often. I was nineteen years old and alone with her when she died. I was holding her hand and it just turned cold. There was nothing I could do. The one thing I wanted to do was find my father, drag him out of whatever bar he had parked himself in and beat him senseless." The boys were shocked to see tears in their father's eyes.

I asked the boys if there was anything they wanted to say to their dad. The son with Down syndrome got up and put his arms around his father. The little one said, "I'm sorry your mom didn't live." The 26-year-old looked his father in the eye and said, "There have been times when I've wanted to drag you out of one of your meetings and hit you, too. I know how you felt." Thomas said, "I can't tell you how sorry I am."

We started to put their joys and sorrows into categories. The joys were playing sports (softball, Thomas' hole-in-

31

one), great theater and pets (Chester the dog). The sadnesses were losing a pet, dealing with diabetes, struggling to establish an acting career, and losing a loved one to cancer.

We proceeded to talk about how they could invest money in the community so that others could share their joy and be spared some of their sadness. Each of them agreed to start looking for organizations that could help people in these ways. Ultimately, the four of them made donations to a number of worthy groups that reflected their concerns and interests: the local chapter of the Humane Society, the Special Olympics, a local scholarship program for golf caddies, and an upstart, non-profit theater company.

After the meeting, Thomas told me that those had been the most meaningful, most difficult three hours he had ever spent with his sons. He felt awful about the divorces, and it was painful to hear about all the things that had brought his sons grief. He was saddened by the time he had spent away from his children while building his corporate empire. While he couldn't cure all the ills of the world, Thomas now saw how he and his sons could help other people, and one another.

Since Thomas and his sons sat down for that first Joy and Sadness Meeting, some things have changed. There is a professional staff running the foundation now—but once a year, Thomas and his sons still get together for what they call "The Meeting of the Men." It is still run as a Joy and Sadness meeting, and Thomas tells me it gets more comfortable for him and his sons every year. Is everything perfect between them? No. Is it better? Absolutely.

How-To Questions

When, where, and with which family members should we hold a Joy and Sadness Meeting?

Pick a date that has meaning for your family. If you traditionally throw a big family barbecue on the Fourth of July, you could incorporate the Joy and Sadness Meeting into that day's activities. If most of the family gathers on Thanksgiving, meet while the turkey is cooking that morning. You could set the date to honor someone's birthday or anniversary, or choose an important date in your family's history, such as when the family first arrived in the United States, or opening day of the family business. You might also want to commemorate a tragedy that has touched your family, such as the death of a loved one. Think of the Joy and Sadness Meeting as an opportunity to share family history and experiences.

Deciding who should attend can be tricky. Once you get more than twelve people, I've found, it becomes difficult for everybody to say what's on their minds and feel involved. Therefore, you might want to keep it to the immediate family, or extend the invitation only to grandparents and grandkids. Then again, if lots of family members want to participate, why not hold more than one Joy and Sadness Meeting? You could have one meeting for the men and one for the women. Or, if the family is spread out geographically, establish East Coast and West Coast chapters.

Avoid dividing up the family by age. Part of the learning experience of a Joy and Sadness Meeting is seeing what concerns are held by different generations and letting the youngsters learn from the adults' behavior. You could, however, institute an age minimum for joining the Joy and Sadness Meeting, which would make it a nice rite of passage.

Hold the meeting at a table (dining room, kitchen or picnic) big enough to accommodate everybody. It is much easier to make group decisions when everybody can see everybody else. This also allows the meeting chairperson to see if somebody appears confused on unhappy—and that's tricky to do when some people are sitting on the couch, some on footstools, and others are sprawled on the floor. If you don't have enough table space at home, see about using a church's or community center's conference room. Sometimes banks will let you use a conference room for free.

What ground rules do we need to set before the meeting?

Great meetings have clear ground rules, which should be set either before the group convenes (over e-mail, for instance) or at the start of the meeting. Rules to determine include:

The length of the meeting. We adults all know how awful it feels to be stuck in a meeting that drags on forever. Imagine how much more restless the little ones will be! When you've reached the end of the pre-allotted meeting time (an hour, I'd recommend), the chair needs to stop the discussion and call a vote on whether or not to extend the meeting, and if so by how long. If that vote doesn't pass by a majority, then the chair needs to call for a vote deciding which charity or cause will receive the family's donation.

Determining who has the floor. You can do this by simple hand-raising, going around the table one by one, or by passing around a "talking stick." The chair must also make sure that everybody gets a chance to voice their opinions before a final vote is held.

Discuss the use of cell phones, pagers, Blackberries, iPods, Sidekicks, walkie-talkies, beeping watches, defibrillators, pacemakers, and other electronic aids. Those first few, you could probably do without.

What is the job of the meeting chairperson, and how should we choose a chair?

Choosing a meeting chair can lead to ego clashes right off the bat, if certain family members always like being in charge, or think that others aren't up to the job. The easiest solutions are drawing straws, or rotating the chair each year alphabetically by first name. Also, institute an age minimum for chairpersons, somewhere between 16 and 21 years old, depending on how maturely the teenagers in your family conduct themselves.

Tasks that need doing during the meeting include taking notes (recording who suggested which charities and why), making sure everybody follows the ground rules, and seeing that discussions don't drag on too long (use an egg timer if you have to). If these seem like too many things for the chair to handle, assign others the roles of secretary and timekeeper.

After each meeting, it is the chair's responsibility to do any further research on potential charities. For example, the family may have narrowed down its targeted benefactor to "a legal-aid group in Detroit," but the chair would need to pinpoint the name of a specific organization. The chair is also responsible for collecting the money and forwarding it to the charity.

How do we get the meeting rolling?

In my family, we start each Joy and Sadness meeting by passing out a list of the charities to which we've donated in the past and why. That's a good way to get people brainstorming about where the current year's donation may be directed. After reading through the list, we then ask ourselves the same question every year: What made you want to cry this year, and what made you want to dance in the streets with joy?

Your chair can decide beforehand what question will be posed at your year's meeting. Whether you stick to one question year in and year out, like my family, or ask a new question each time, beware of asking too many questions at a single meeting. The meeting will never end!

Below are some good sample questions, or you can make up your own.

What made you happy in the past year?

What made you sad in the past year?

Where do you turn to for information and news?

Who has been the most influential person in your life, and why?

If you could have changed anything in the world this year, what would it have been?

What is your favorite place to visit?

If you could help only one person, who would it be and why?

If you could change anything about yourself, what would it be and why?

What lesson did you learn in the past year?

What frightened you this year?

How much money should we earmark toward the charities we choose?

Some families might decide that all of the adults will chip in equal amounts; others might decide to have only one monetary donor. Children with allowances or jobs can be asked to contribute as well. All of this depends on how much money people feel comfortable donating. If the adults in your family don't want to discuss finances in front of the children, settle this beforehand over phone or e-mail.

Remember that the point of the Joy and Sadness Meeting is not how much money you round up from individual relatives; it's about doing something charitable as a family, year in and year out. Making sure everybody feels happy and comfortable with the amount they give is much more important than the actual dollar amount.

How can we wrap up the meeting efficiently?

In my family, the chair ends each meeting by asking each person to summarize the meeting out loud, saying what he or she thinks did or didn't work. The kind of responses we frequently hear begin, "I was so surprised to hear that..." or "I didn't know that..." or "Thank you for sharing your thoughts on...". Such declarations reaffirm for us that the Joy and

Sadness Meeting not only improves the lives of those we help monetarily—it also brings us closer together as a family.

How can we make this meeting fun and comfortable for everybody?

It can be hard to keep the younger kids' attention during the Joy and Sadness Meeting. One way to remedy that—and also to teach those youngsters about money and charity—is to make play money available to them during the meeting, and use it to illustrate how donations work.

Also, remember that food and music make any occasion special. Couples always have "our song," and some entertainers and professional speakers (like me) have their own theme music. (Mine is Donna Summer's "She Works Hard for the Money."). Why not a theme song for your family, too? I'd suggest the theme from *Rocky*, Aretha Franklin's "Respect" or one of my favorites, Joe Cocker singing "With a Little Help from My Friends."

Serve a family-favorite dish or drink as well. My family loves hot mulled cider with a clove-studded orange and a few cinnamon sticks bobbing around in it, which makes our kitchen smell wonderful. As one of my sons said when he was little, "Hot cider makes my nose happy." I've found that, after cooking all day on Thanksgiving—the day we hold our annual Joy and Sadness Meeting—hot mulled cider with a splash of rum makes all of me happy!

Grandma's Birthday Gift

The Big Question: How can holidays, birthdays and other special occasions serve as learning opportunities about the joys of giving?

I recently gave a keynote address to a convention of non-profit volunteers, in which I mentioned this very book. After my talk, a plump, elderly woman named Marcy came up to me and said, "So, you're writing a book on how to raise charitable children? Can I buy you a cup of coffee? I have some ideas I'd like to share." There was a Starbucks in the hotel lobby where we could sit and talk, but Marcy said, "Forget it, the pastries at Starbucks are lousy. Let's have our coffee in the hotel dining room." Clearly, Marcy was my kind of woman—I'm a sucker for fresh, fancy pastries.

After we settled in with our coffee and much-tastier-than-Starbucks scones, Marcy told me her story. She began, "I grew up in a loving, middle-class family where everybody had plenty of everything. My husband, however, endured a different upbringing. Stan was a child of the Depression who'd fought for everything he had.

"We met when I was volunteering at a USO on the East Coast during WWII. I fell madly in love with him. He was handsome, and he had what they call 'street smarts.' We wrote to one another while he was stationed overseas. Stan had such big dreams, but he wasn't well-educated. He'd ask me to correct the grammar and spelling mistakes in his letters and send them back to him. Can you imagine such a thing?

"When he came back from the war, we married. My family was appalled; I was a college graduate, but he hadn't even risen to the rank of officer in the service. I had a little money from an aunt who'd died, and Stan and I used it to start a salvage business. Our first days were difficult, but I was very, very happy. I kept the books for the business, and when our first child came along, we set up a crib in a corner of the office for him. We had a second son and, eventually, we became quite wealthy. Our sons are grown now, and I have a grandson and a granddaughter. One of my sons lives near me with his wife and daughter; my other son is divorced and lives with his son hundreds of miles away. Stan died nine years ago."

Marcy stopped talking. A tear made a trail through the powder on her face. She dabbed her cheek with a linen napkin, took a deep breath, and continued. "Anyway, back to the kids. My sons have lived privileged lives. Frankly, they take everything for granted. Then along came my grandchildren, who are totally overindulged. I get along well with my children, but I do try to keep my mouth shut about how they raise their kids."

But one year, when Marcy's granddaughter Deborah was four years old, Marcy tried something different.

Deborah asked Marcy what she wanted for her upcoming birthday. Marcy came up with a brilliant idea. She replied, "Do something for someone else, draw me a picture illustrating what you did, and then tell me the story behind the picture on my birthday."

Several weeks later, Deborah showed up at her grandma's birthday party with a somewhat confusing picture. Marcy said, "Tell me about your wonderful coloring." Deborah explained, "Mommy was in the bathroom and forgot her towel. I went to the basement all by myself and got it out of the dryer. This is me carrying it up the stairs to Mommy. I don't like going into the basement alone, but I went."

Marcy and Deborah started talking about how you sometimes have to do things you're afraid of in order to help others. Marcy went to her jewelry box and retrieved the Purple Heart that Stan had been awarded during WWII. She showed it to Deborah, and they talked about how brave Stan had been during his tour of duty. Then Marcy told Deborah how proud she was that Deborah had conquered her fears, and that her grandfather would have been proud of her as well.

The next year, Marcy and Deborah started keeping a scrapbook together, containing Deborah's pictures and stories, as well as some professionally-done photographs of the two of them. I asked Marcy what her son and daughter-in-law thought of this new annual project. She said they liked it so much, they'd even offered to become involved with it themselves. Marcy asked that they adopt a supportive role.

Deborah is now nine years old. For Marcy's most recent birthday, she collected 800 pounds of food for a homeless shelter. Deborah wrote a story telling how others had responded when she asked for food donations, and what the folks at the shelter had said when she and her father showed up with an SUV full of food.

Marcy's son suggested that, after that experience, she might want to spare his back and just ask for perfume for her next birthday. Marcy smiled and said, "Dear, I will buy my own perfume. This is working just fine."

I asked Marcy about her other grandchild, Jeffrey. "Does he do the same kind of good deeds in honor of your birthday?" Marcy sighed and said that although she's asked, neither Jeffrey nor his dad think it's a good idea.

"I just can't seem to connect with Jeffrey," she explained. "He is 12 years old now and everything he does involves a screen. I mean, he has three computers and a cell phone, and whenever we're together, all he wants to do is play video games. I worry that Jeffrey is disconnected from people. I love to volunteer with Meals On Wheels and sit and visit with people. Jeffrey would rather interact with a screen than a person."

Listening to her despair about her grandson, I got an idea. "If your grandson loves screens," I suggested to her, "why not ask him to build a website for one of the small non-profits you support?"

Suddenly she looked up and said, "You know, that Jeffrey would do. I think I've been asking him for the wrong thing. I've been asking him to connect with people the way I do, not the way he does. I'm going to call Jeffrey tonight."

Marcy and I spent two hours talking like strangers on a train; we never even thought to exchange last names. But we did exchange valuable ideas about improving our relationships with the children in our families. As we wrapped up our conversation, Marcy said enthusiastically, "I love it. Now I have a way to make Jeffrey a part of this project that is so important to me. I want to reach out to him. I do love that little stinker."

My birthday came six weeks after I met Marcy. Following her lead, when my niece asked me what I wanted for my birthday, I told her to do something for someone else and write it up for me. Thanks to Marcy, I have a marvelous memory, as does the person who was helped by my niece. It's a much better present than watermelon-scented bath oil!

How-To Questions

Which special occasions are good opportunities for kids to do charity and volunteer work?

Obviously, there are birthdays, as well as "the big" holidays such as Christmas, Thanksgiving, and Hanukkah. For any one of these special days, a child can be asked to perform an act of charity, similar to what Deborah did for her grandmother, as a gift on behalf of a loved one. But other holidays like Labor Day, Independence Day and Memorial Day might have great significance for your family and could provide valuable opportunities for learning and contributing as well.

If that's the case, make time for your child to talk to Uncle Ralph about his service in the Gulf War, or to Grandma about her days in the WAVES, and then suggest your child do something helpful to honor that part of your family's history. To commemorate Veterans Day, for instance, you and your kids might bake brownies to take to the local Veterans of Foreign Wars hall.

How can I get other adults who are involved in my child's life to consider asking for such gifts?

Encourage your child to phone a relative with an upcoming birthday, anniversary, or other special occasion, and ask what he or she could do in their honor. (Usually, adults are floored when a child asks what he or she can do for them for a change!)

If the adult isn't sure how to respond, ask him or her to simply name a favorite charity. If a grandparent is very involved at the church, for example, you can call the church and see if there's something there that needs doing. It can be an hour of babysitting in the church's pre-school or simply sorting the hymnals. Get creative with the ways your child can contribute—and as always, the more involved the child is in making the act of charity happen, the better.

How can I teach my child the importance of philanthropy even when we buy a gift for somebody?

Shopping is one of my great loves, and when I can, I like to support the retail outlets at my favorite charities. Museum shops are perfect for this sort of thing. If your family recently enjoyed a trip to the Smithsonian, browse their online shop when you and your child are looking for birthday or holiday gifts for friends and family. Explain how charities are funded, and that by purchasing gifts from their store, you are supporting the charity's mission.

What if a child, like Marcy's grandson, is reluctant to take on a charity project when I've asked him or her to do so?

These days, with their backpacks bursting at the seams with homework and their schedules booked solid with extracurriculars, children can wind up feeling just as overwhelmed as adults. As a child's aunt, uncle, or grandparent— or even as his or her mom or dad—you may not fully know what's going on in a child's life that would make him or her resist taking on such a project.

So try a little negotiating. Ask for just three hours of a child's time, and ask that it be spent in any way that would benefit the two of you and others. The child can decide which specifics task to take on—filing or answering phones at a start-up arts organization, mowing grass or doing laundry at a local women's shelter—and what would be the best time to fit the volunteer project into his or her schedule. If afterschool hours and weekends won't work, suggest holding off on it until he or she has got some vacation time, even if that means waiting a few months.

If you're still not getting anywhere with the kid, start even smaller. If the local zoo is one of your favorite charities, ask the child to simply accompany you on an afternoon excursion there, and say that his or her presence is present enough. Once there, take the time to talk about how zoos operate and how they rely on donations of both time and money from people just like you. You could also get the child to start thinking about the importance of philanthropy by posing a few hypothetical questions, such as "If someone gave you one million dollars and told you that you couldn't spend any of it on yourself, what would you do with the money?"

What you want most out of this gift is for the child to develop a better understanding of who you are and what you value. As a bonus, perhaps he or she will realize that spending 20 minutes at the mall, or five minutes browsing the Internet, doesn't make for a very special gift after all.

The Big Question: How can I put together a group volunteering project for my child and his or her friends that will prove fun and rewarding for them—while not driving myself insane at the same time?

If you're a kid who calls Epworth Children & Family Services in Webster Groves, Missouri, your home, then your first home probably wasn't a great one. A 140-year-old residential treatment center for disturbed adolescents, Epworth takes in troubled teenagers and preteens who have often endured violent and abusive parents, lived in foster homes, or had problems with drugs. Almost all of them were in the custody of the state before being sent to Epworth.

Such children might seem like the worst possible candidates for a weeklong group volunteer project. But every summer, Reverend Rachel Williams—a member of the

49

Epworth staff known by the kids as "Pastor Rachel"—not only chaperones such undertakings successfully, but does so while taking them out of their familiar habitats into places unknown.

Pastor Rachel and her charges have helped clean and refurbish senior citizens' houses in Springfield, Missouri, renovated an inner-city church in Chicago, and repaired a community center on a Native American reservation in South Dakota. They have stripped paint off walls, applied fresh coats of paint, torn down dilapidated ceilings, installed dry wall and bathroom floors, done yard work, and vacuumed people's living rooms. These were tasks that none of the children had ever attempted before.

As if that weren't asking enough, the kids (who travel by chaperoned campus van) rarely stay in hotels or eat prepared meals while on their volunteer trips. In Springfield, they slept in sleeping bags on a church's gym floor and cooked for themselves every night. In South Dakota, they bunked inside a community house that didn't have a television or even a basketball court. As Rex, one of the kids on that excursion, puts it, "All we had was lights and electricity." And usually, there are only three or four Epworth kids of the 20 or so teenagers in attendance; the rest are "regular" kids who participate through their churches' youth groups. Sometimes the Epworth kids are also the only people of color.

Yet year after year, these projects go off without a hitch. In addition to the service work they do on these trips, the kids enjoy a planned day of fun—they've gone swimming, attended an amusement park, even visited Mount Rushmore—and Pastor Rachel experiences no problems with them on those outings, either.

The "volunteer vacations" are not the Epworth children's only opportunities to experience the joy of helping others.

During the school year, Pastor Rachel takes them on day-long, locally-based community service projects one Saturday a month. Whereas getting to go away for the weeklong projects depends on a child's age and how far along in the Epworth program he or she has progressed, these local excursions are open to all Epworth kids between the ages of eleven and seventeen; all they have to do is put their names down on a sign-up sheet beforehand. On these afternoons, the children have painted a nursery school, served pancakes at a homeless shelter, cleaned toys for a new day-care center, walked dogs at animal shelters, and helped rehab private homes. (Needless to say, knocking down walls was a favorite activity for them.) After these day-long projects, Pastor Rachel takes the kids out for some pizza or ice cream as a way to both reward and refuel them.

The immediate and long-lasting benefits of these projects—whether week-long or day-long—are obvious. Thirteen-year-old Alex, who went on the Springfield trip, originally wanted to go "just because there are different people there." He now says, "I think the skills will help me in a new foster home." Alex also noticed how appreciative the senior citizens were of the kids' help. "One woman ordered us pizza and made us fresh-squeezed lemonade. She took, like, an hour and a half to make the lemonade. I was like, man, that's nice. It made me feel better than what I usually do with my time."

Adds 15-year-old John, who was brought to Epworth after he was caught doing drugs, "I'd do the volunteer projects millions of times. It's something to do besides just staying home, playing video games and looking like a zombie."

Pastor Rachel admits that many kids initially sign up just so they have a reason to get off campus or take a vacation.

But, she says, "By the end of the project, they'll say to me, 'That was fun,' which I think is their way of saying that it felt good to help somebody else."

She also believes that the kids' exposure to different peer groups on the weeklong trips helps them on their road to recovery and maturity. "The other kids on these trips can be really rich and smart and well-behaved. When our kids go on these trips, you see the best of them. Their behavior mirrors the kids around them."

"Most importantly," says Pastor Rachel, "doing these projects gets them out of their ruts. These kids don't come from anything, but in doing volunteer work they start to realize that other people have it bad, too. Everything seems so futile to them most of the time, but this shows them that they have the capacity to make other people's lives better, which means maybe their lives can get better, too."

How-To Questions

How do I start looking for a volunteer project that a group of kids can do together?

Before you start searching for volunteer opportunities, you have to be very clear about what your group can handle. Talk to the other kids' parents and find out their children's talents, skills and limitations: How much time does a child have on a Saturday afternoon to volunteer? Does he or she get tired or cranky after a certain amount of time? Can the child handle a bit of physical labor, such as sorting and stacking cases of food, or doing clean-up work? Might he or she get nervous around stray animals, older adults, or the hospitalized?

It's equally important to find out certain things about the other parents. Will they have time to help organize and/or chaperone a volunteer project? (Important: How big a group you wind up with should depend first and foremost on how much supervision you are able to provide. You might want to start small with your first project—say, five or so kids—and then work your way up from there.) Does one of the parents know somebody at a non-profit organization who can provide an "in" to a project? Are they OK with their children being exposed to certain situations, such as encountering homeless people while helping out at a soup kitchen?

There are some types of volunteer projects that suit almost any young group. They can help out with envelope stuffing for a nonprofit's mass mailing (see below for tips on making such a potentially boring project fun), or sing Christmas carols in a hospital ward or assisted-living facility, especially if the group shares some talent for singing or playing instruments.

What kinds of group volunteer projects do kids usually like best?

Let the kids answer this question. Schedule a brainstorming session for them to name some of the societal concerns they have. This list might include homelessness, animals, the environment, AIDS, other health issues and so forth. The answers will vary based on what's going on in their lives and in the media. Whittle that list down to two or three specific volunteer projects that speak to those concerns, and let the kids vote on those. One thing that will help get kids excited about volunteering is giving them some choice in the matter—but don't present them with an open-ended question like, "What should we do as a volunteer project?" You will have mayhem!

Overall, kids tend to like projects that connect to the mission of an organization. They like knowing that the work they are doing helps the mission. One popular choice for active kids is an "a-thon" event, such as a bike-a-thon, walk-a-thon, skate-a-thon, etc. The kids become involved in raising money for the cause, and they also get to see how many other people just like them care enough about the cause to do something about it. If you are doing an "a-thon," though, take the time to really discuss the cause behind the event. You might want to ask the organization you are raising funds for if someone can talk to your group before the event, or at the very least send some literature the children can read and comprehend. This will help the kids' fundraising efforts, because they'll be equipped to effectively describe to potential donors why the cause is important.

A nine-year-old neighbor of mine once came to my door collecting money for a breast cancer walk. I asked her, "Why do you think this is important?" She said, "My Aunt Julia had breast cancer and it really hurts when you throw up. It's a genetic disease and I can get it like my aunt. I have to get breasts first, but I'm walking now." Her answer made me rush into the house to get my checkbook!

What ages fare best in different kinds of volunteering environments?

A group of eight-year-olds would be great at making sandwiches for a food pantry or decorating wreaths with seniors at a nursing home. However, you would not be able to bring them to a pediatric oncology unit to play with toddlers, or to a battered women's shelter to install windows—though an older group of mid- to late-teen volunteers should be able to handle those projects.

Older children, whom I define as 12 and up, can get much more involved in the decision-making process, as well as researching volunteer opportunities. Teenagers can do the online and phone research needed to find locally-based projects. Ask them what they think is a major problem in your community—then ask them what they think they can do to help alleviate it. This is a very pro-active stance for them to take, and it can teach them about self-reliance and creative problem-solving. For instance, if the group decides to focus on a community's lack of recreation facilities for young kids, they can figure out how to raise funds for a new playground (which they'll then help construct, of course!) or how to organize an after-school program (which they'll then help supervise!).

What if a charity wants us to do something boring?

If your group is asked to do a rote project, such as stuffing envelopes, you might want to consider a ritual practiced in the cigar factories of Cuba and have a "reader." The reader entertains the cigar rollers (or, in your case, envelope stuffers) by reading aloud from a book. Whether you choose the latest Harry Potter, or a book that is related to the cause you are supporting, the time will pass much more quickly.

How big of a group should we invite?

You can have enormous numbers of kids involved in the project if—and only if!—you have enough work, adults, transportation, food, bathrooms and space to accommodate them all. Always check with an agency beforehand to find out how much childpower they'll need for a certain project, whether they'll be able to provide some supervision, and whether there's room enough for the kids to do the work—you don't need to take 80 kids to wash 15 dogs at an animal shelter.

The larger the group, the greater the need you'll find for a division of labor. So if you're volunteering at an animal shelter, one team of kids can wash the dogs, another team will haul and stock bags of dog food, and another team will help file paperwork. You can rotate teams so that everybody gets a chance to do everything.

Generally, with children under 12, you will want at least one adult per five children. If you have a mature group that has worked together before, you can raise that ratio somewhat.

How do I best supervise the kids while they're working?

Supervision is not just about making sure the work gets done. It is also about preventing problems and emotionally debriefing the kids when necessary. Once, when a friend's daughter was volunteering with a group at a retirement home, an elderly Alzheimer's patient grabbed her bottom. The girl, age 14, was about to hit the old man—she was so surprised that it was just an automatic response—when a nurse stopped her. The nurse took her into the hallway to talk about it. The girl had been frightened and upset at first, but was relieved once the nurse explained to her that the man's action was unintentional.

Feeding the kids is a key issue too, probably more than you might realize. You need to feed and water your young volunteers. Adults get crabby when they haven't been adequately nourished and so do kids. This is particularly true during after-school time, when blood sugar drops and tempers rise.

Ask the organization you're helping if they provide snacks or if you should bring them. With the rise of diabetes in children, plus the inevitable crash after a sugar rush, you don't want to provide snacks that are super-high in sugar. Allergies are another thing to consider; ask each child's parent if he or she suffers from any. And finally, make sure it won't be a problem to serve your goodies at the volunteer site. This is particularly important if you go to a Jewish or Muslim site, where dietary laws preclude certain foods from being brought on the premises. Sitting down for a snack at an animal shelter, homeless shelter, soup kitchen or hospital ward might also be inappropriate. In those cases, ask about arranging a separate place for the kids to eat. (Often at soup kitchens, volunteers are welcome to fix themselves a plate from the cafeteria line after they're done working, and to eat among the soup kitchen's guests. This can prove an invaluable opportunity for children to learn about poverty and home-lessness on a very personal, up-close level.)

So, what snacks should you bring? Crackers, cheese and fruit are always great. My husband, Frank, always recommends bananas because "they have appeal." (Our family has long since stopped laughing at this joke, but you might find it amusing.)

What are the pros and cons of doing a one-time service project compared to an ongoing volunteer experience?

Obviously, the one-shot deal works best if you can only assemble a group of kids for a single time period. The group can try to meet once a month, or once every three months, or what have you to do volunteer work, but maybe not the exact same group every time. You certainly don't want the headache that comes from promising a charity that five kids will show up, and instead three or ten do. Also, a one-time experience lets you "test" the volunteer program to see if it's a good fit for both the agency and the kids; if it is, you can always see about making it a recurring activity.

Ongoing work often means your group becomes of greater service to the charity, and the children learn not just about the cause they're helping, but also about the rewards that come from commitment and endurance.

What kind of thanks or recognition should we give the children after they've completed their project?

Although donating one's time should always be regarded as reward unto itself, kids, like adults, appreciate positive reinforcement. Also like adults, children only have so much discretionary time and energy. To want to get involved in charitable work again, recognition is a great motivator. You needn't hire a band and bestow medals every time the kids do something charitable, but recognition is important when the kids are starting a new volunteer project, or perhaps have just completed a long-term one.

As the adult involved, check with the charity beforehand regarding what kind of a volunteer recognition program they may have. Some, like the Red Cross, are wonderfully well organized and seasoned at not only tracking volunteers' hours, but also thanking volunteers graciously, inexpensively, and often. Such a group can offer the children shirts and caps for their labor. Other younger, smaller organizations might be struggling just to keep their doors open and therefore lack the resources for creating some sort of recognition. If this is the case, by all means take it upon yourself to make sure the children's work is recognized.

Different kinds of kids will want different kinds of recognition. College-bound high school kids may want a letter for their college applications. For kids involved in the juvenile justice system, a letter to their guardian ad litem or judge might be welcome. For younger kids, a photo in the paper will probably thrill them!

To Haiti with Love

The Big Question: How can we get more out of a family vacation than just a sunburn?

When Missouri Supreme Court Justice Michael Wolff was running for state attorney general about 15 years ago, he told a campaign worker that he and his wife, Pat, were taking their eleven- and fourteen-year-old sons on a two-week volunteering trip to Haiti. The campaign worker replied, "Why don't you just have them eat ground glass?"

Indeed, why on earth would two well-to-do, mentally competent parents who had never done volunteer work like this before—and had never even been to Haiti themselves—decide to take their children on such a vacation? Explains Pat, "The kids were turning into whining, entitled Americans. They were wondering why they didn't have a big-screen TV, and what was up with living in the same house all year. And besides, we'd already been to Disney World."

So after one too many times of feeding their kids the old line "You know, there are starving children in other parts of the world," Pat and Mike finally decided to take their kids to see the starving children.

For two weeks, the Wolffs lived at a boys' orphanage in Port-au-Prince, paying rent for the privilege. Some days, they volunteered at Mother Teresa's Home for Dying Children, where they fed, bathed, and played with the young patients. Other days, they visited Mother Teresa's Home for Dying Adults, where they simply spent time being good company to those who lived there, engaging in friendly conversation and providing back rubs. The family ate rice and beans twice a day, cooked by the boys living in the orphanage.

Pat and Mike realized that a number of worst-case scenarios could happen to them on their trip: a serious bus accident, robbery, rape, drowning at sea. Reflecting back on the experience today, Pat says, "We had lots of anxiety, but we prepared the best we could. And we decided to live by our hopes rather than our fears."

Instead of packing suntan oil and beach books for their summer vacation, the Wolffs brought bottles of albumin, saline drip and empty blood bags—in case Pat, a pediatrician, needed to perform an emergency blood transfusion from one family member to another due to a serious accident. Pat and Mike also purchased evacuation insurance before the trip.

The Wolffs witnessed things in Haiti they'd never seen before, like raw-sewage canals and dead bodies in the streets. But they also saw something even more shocking: smiling faces. Says Andy, the older son, "What really stood out was that there were a lot of people who were happy. This trip taught me that people who don't have a lot of things can be equally as happy as people who do."

Even though Pat worked as a pediatrician back home, her medical expertise wasn't needed in Haiti—not for any family emergency, as it turned out, and not for the terminally ill people they met there, either. The family's work was mainly to offer comfort and solace.

The boys often carried out the smallest tasks—fetching rags and passing out medicine—but younger son Ben says he never remembers feeling unimportant or helpless there. "I knew that I was just contributing a little bit," he says today, "but that I was also doing what I could."

When they came home, Ben and Andy never again complained about not having enough stuff. This vacation put a total end to their absorption with things. Andy remembers returning home and "feeling struck by the fact that I could drink water out of the faucet. I'd never realized before what a big plus that was. The trip really gave me an appreciation for my station in life." (Ben also remembers coming home and "really appreciating non-iodized water.")

Says Pat, "After the trip, the kids understood what we meant when we'd tell them that we didn't want to waste money on this or that. We may have money, but let's not throw it away on stupid stuff because we could use it better, in Haiti or elsewhere."

Five years later, Pat and Andy went back to Haiti together for one week, to work in another village. Andy returned by himself for the next two years after that, volunteering as a surgical assistant in a hospital.

Andy, now 30, works as an orthopedic surgery resident at Yale; he is the husband of an OB-GYN resident and the father of a toddler. Ben spent two years after college working as an investigator in the public defender's office in the Bronx, and another ten months living in Nicaragua, in a house where the walls didn't go all the way up to the ceiling, learning Spanish and working with teenage gangs. He now attends law school at Berkeley and plans to go into public-interest law.

Today, Andy claims that those trips "inspired me to choose a profession where I could help people. It also gave me a close-up view of what my Mom did for a living, and it gave me a greater understanding of just how poor the conditions are in the Third World."

How-To Questions

How do I talk to my family about taking a volunteer vacation?

The question that never comes up when discussing a family vacation—whether a "regular" or a volunteer vacation— is, "What do we want to get out of our trip?" This question is a great place to start such a discussion.

The best family vacations happen when you do something very different from your normal, everyday life. Other than poorer, how do you, as a family, want to be different after returning home? Do you want to be rested, or energized? Educated? Spiritually nourished? Tan? Inspired? Thinner? Fitter? Fatter? Closer as a family?

Are there talents you want to develop, such as home-building and repair, gardening and forestry, or speaking a foreign language? Are there talents your family already has that you want to share with others?

Think about the opposite of your everyday lives and how you can live that out in a volunteer vacation. This will not only broaden your horizons; doing something totally different will appeal to children's sense of adventure. City dwellers might want to consider volunteering at a national park or forest. A family of ranchers, who normally engages in lots of physical labor, could teach reading to inner-city kids for a change of pace.

You can also spark a child's interest in a volunteer vacation by tying it into pop culture. Whatever's hot in TV, movies and games—*George of the Jungle, March of the Penguins, The Amazing Race,* etc.—there's a trip and a volunteer project to match. After all, a vacation is like a little bit of Harry Potter—without the wand.

How can I find a suitable volunteer vacation for my family?

While the Wolffs arranged their trip through a small, loosely organized group called The Haiti Project, these days a surprising number of reputable non-profit associations and placement agencies have pre-planned volunteer vacations available. Many of these groups you've probably already heard of—like Habitat for Humanity International or the Sierra Club—while others are lesser known because they work on a smaller scale, such as Global Volunteers or Volunteers for Peace. (These and additional volunteer-vacation organizations are listed in this book's Resources chapter. You can also check them out on my website, www.raisingcharitablechildren.com.) Most of these groups offer package-style vacations, providing accommodations, meals, itineraries, tools and instructors.

Given the wide range of choices out there, you and your family can scale down the possibilities by asking yourselves questions like:

How "rustic" are you? Could the whole family tolerate living in tents for a week, or going without showering?

Are the kids big and strong enough to handle things like hammering or heavy lifting?

Does anybody in the family speak a foreign language?

Does anybody have a medical condition that could become a problem in certain locales or climates?

Is there a certain part of the country or the world you've always wanted to see up close?

Is there a particular cause you're strongly drawn to, like protecting an endangered species or stopping the spread of AIDS in Africa?

For most volunteer-vacation opportunities, though, all that's really needed is a desire to help. If you're willing to put in the time and effort, any number of organizations will help you find a vacation that suits you and your family, even if you've never picked up a screwdriver or pulled up a weed in your life.

To get started, browse through a few volunteer-vacation websites, then request more information by mail for those specific trips that catch your eye.

Another resource I highly recommend is the book *Volunteer Vacations: Short-Term Adventures That Will Benefit You and Others,* written by Bill McMillon and published by Chicago Review Press.

How much will the trip cost?

Transportation expenses to and from the volunteer site are rarely, if ever, covered by the non-profit agencies that administer these volunteer vacations. You'll be responsible for arranging and paying for any and all travel costs on your own.

Almost always, a volunteer vacation will also carry a fee (usually partially or fully tax-deductible; make sure to check) that you'll pay directly to the non-profit organization, ranging anywhere from fifty to a few thousand dollars. This usually covers things like food, accommodations, and any materials or equipment you might use in carrying out your volunteer work. The fee might also include a monetary donation to help offset the group's administrative costs.

Obviously, if you're pitching your own tent in a national park and eating cookout food while helping restore trails for the American Hiking Society, your costs to the group won't be that high. But other trips may come with translators, security personnel, prepared meals, hotel rooms, etc., and will therefore cost more.

Just like with regular vacations, there truly are volunteer vacations to fit any budget. You can always stick close to home to cut down on travel costs. Some volunteer vacations are scheduled for certain dates and lengths of time, but with others you can be flexible about the length of your stay, which can also reduce your costs.

If you can't travel, consider an "in-town" volunteer vacation. You can save on transportation and skip the packing! No matter where you live, there is almost always a completely different culture within spitting distance where you can make a contribution. Plus, you'll be showing your kids that you don't need a train, plane or automobile in order to be somebody who can make a difference.

How should we prepare ourselves for the trip?

The more wildly different your choice of vacation vis-à-vis your normal life, the more preparation and training you'll need to do. Physical training beforehand is usually very important; it will prevent injury to yourself, thus allowing you to be more helpful to others.

Say you'll be working on renovating a school, but you and your spouse are veteran desk jockeys, and your kids aren't athletic types. Doing some strength-training workouts at the gym beforehand wouldn't be a bad idea—otherwise, there won't be enough Ben-Gay in the world to treat your aching muscles during your vacation.

If you're going to be doing some housepainting, do a practice run with the whole family before you go. (You might even turn that into another volunteer project in your hometown.) Make sure everybody's comfortable on high ladders. If you're going to help clean up part of a national park, you'll probably be doing a lot of walking, so start a family walking regimen to get acclimated to the extra exercise. Also, teach kids how to lift things properly (bend from the knees!) before they engage in manual labor.

Cultural differences also require preparation—for the sake of your own family, as well as the people you'll be working with and helping. You don't want anybody behaving in a gauche fashion when exposed to these different populations, especially if you're working with the young, sick or elderly. You also don't want your children to be overly alarmed by the new culture. Read the kids bedtime stories about the place you'll be visiting. Look at maps with them. If you're going to a place where a foreign language is spoken, teach them how to say things like "hello," "thank you," and "please" in that language.

When it comes to packing for the trip, think long and hard about the things you need to bring—and especially, the things not to bring. It's amazing what you don't really need in this world. (Any Hurricane Katrina survivor can tell you that.) Check with the organization you're working for about what you'll need and what they'll supply for you (food, first-aid supplies, sleeping bags, towels, etc.).

One crucial reminder: Always bring bug spray! Especially if you're the kind of tasty delight that I am. Bug bites can singlehandedly ruin a vacation. Another crucial reminder: A jar of peanut butter and a box of crackers can go a long way when you're roughing it in the woods, or when you're in a foreign place and your kids aren't liking the local cuisine.

When a Twig Catches Fire

The Big Question: When my kid comes home with an enormous, inspired idea to change the world, how can I help him or her realize that goal when our family has limited time and money?

Susie Temkin had been a library hound since her preschool days, and by the time she reached adolescence, she was working at a local library branch in her hometown of Miami, Florida. While on the job, Susie began to notice that fewer and fewer kids there were actually reading books, opting instead to entertain themselves with the library's computers and videos. Determined to lure them back to books, Susie took matters into her own hands: She decided to create a newsletter for kids that combined the fun of games and puzzles with her love of reading, and she planned to distribute a new edition every month at the library where she worked.

When Susie first told her parents, Maria and Ron, that she wanted to produce a newsletter, they were instantly supportive. Like their daughter, Maria and Ron were both big-time bookworms. Maria was a historic preservationist by training who eventually became a library cataloguer, while Ron, an attorney, loved reading about history.

Susie's parents also knew what it was like to be involved in philanthropy. In fact, the adults in the extended Temkin family had a tradition of jointly donating college scholarship money to underprivileged teenagers. Maria had also started up the Sunday school program at their church.

Maria offered to edit the first draft of Susie's newsletter. When it was ready to go to press, Ron Xeroxed a few copies at his office.

It was during the distribution phase that Susie encountered her first roadblock. The newsletter was initially turned down by the library, because they already had other programs in place to encourage reading among children.

Susie was understandably discouraged, but Maria explained to her that, in trying to distribute her newsletter, she was stepping on other people's toes and asking people to adjust their routines for her sake.

So Susie went back to the drawing board. To make her newsletter more appealing, she decided to tie its monthly content into an upcoming holiday like Thanksgiving or Valentine's Day. She went back to the library and showed them her reformatted newsletter. Eventually, the library administrators started showing interest, realizing how they could incorporate her newsletter into their own literacy programming.

Before long, Susie's newsletter circulation expanded to include two elementary schools and an after-school program. She continued doing theme issues; one of her

72

most popular was the Harry Potter issue she put together in conjunction with the debut of the first Harry Potter movie.

As Susie settled into a production routine, so did her parents. Her mother edited all of Susie's newsletters, and her father did most of the chauffeuring to the copy store and the schools and libraries. Her parents paid for her copies, which they say didn't amount to much.

Says Ron today about the help he and Maria gave Susie, "I find it very frustrating when adults don't want to be bothered helping their kids help other people." In fact, when Susie left home to attend college at Duke University, her younger sister took over some of her charity work, and Ron willingly reprised his driving duties all over again.

Looking back, Maria thinks that Susie learned about more than just fonts and layout. "She learned how institutions work, or don't work. She learned how to circumvent the established rules to do something she really believed in. She definitely learned about tenacity."

But Susie's teenage philanthropic tendencies still weren't sated. Next, she started donating children's books and craft supplies to the places that distributed her newsletter, and did craft projects on-site with the kids at the after-school program. Her parents again helped her pay for those materials, which they again say didn't cost much at all.

Then Susie started up a totally different charity effort. She began collecting sample sizes of hygiene products—like the shampoos, soaps and conditioners that come free in hotel rooms. She grouped them into baskets, and gave them to the Miami Rescue Mission for the victims of domestic violence who sought shelter there.

Susie's whole family got involved in her second effort. Her grandmother and aunt started collecting products wherever they went, and asked their friends and neighbors to collect them as well. Susie's aunt, Terrie Temkin, once went a little overboard when returning from a 21-day trip to Australia. As always, she'd felt compelled to bring home as many toiletries as she could from the hotels she'd stayed in, asking for extras from the housekeeping staff and collecting them from other hotel guests. She wound up having to pay $100 at the airport for her overweight baggage—it would have cost her less to buy the same amount of toiletries from a drugstore back in the U.S.! But Terrie, like all of Susie's adult relatives, knew how important it was to support her project. Kids always see the generosity of their parents and loved ones.

In her senior year of high school, Susie won an award from Nestle called Very Best in Youth, commemorating her charitable projects. She got to go to California to receive the award and toured Universal Studios. Susie's grandmother flew out to California to be with her. Nestle also donated $2000 on Susie's behalf to the charity of her choice.

Says Susie, "I couldn't have done this at all without my parents. They knew a lot more about the resources out there." The Temkin family has always been close—now that Susie is at Duke, she still talks to her parents every day—and sometimes they have different opinions. But her parents knew that when it came to Susie's charity work, the best thing they could do for her, says Maria, was "to get out of her way and let her do what she wanted."

74

How-To Questions

How can I help my child devise a game plan for making his or her philanthropic vision come true?

To give your child's overall vision some shape, start by sitting down together and posing the following questions:

Who are we going to contact first?

There may very well be an already-existing agency or organization dedicated to the need your child wants to address. Finding out about and getting in touch with them would be a perfect first step to see how your child may be able to contribute, much like Susie teamed up with the local library to make her dream a reality.

If nobody else in your area seems to be addressing your child's chosen cause, then you need to devise of a list of the people you and your child want on your "team": neighbors, friends, classmates, fellow Scouts, those with experience in a related field, the Parent Teacher Association, etc. Think big. This is a time to create your dream team. The worst that can happen by asking people to join your cause is that they will say no. Ask any salesperson; although none of them love hearing "no," few, if any, have died from it.

Another group of people you should think about contacting is the media. Whether it's the local paper, People magazine, or both, a little publicity can go a long way for a newfound charity. And most jaded reporters would be tickled pink to receive a call from a precocious, philanthropic eight-year-old looking for a little coverage.

What kinds of resources and supplies do we think we'll need?

Soliciting for in-kind donations is always easier than asking people for money. So when brainstorming a list of the raw materials your child will need—be it paper, canned goods, gardening supplies, etc.—think first about how you can obtain them for free. Besides hitting up friends, coworkers and relatives for in-kind donations, you can post requests for items on websites like craigslist.org and freecycle.org, where people give away or sell on the cheap all kinds of useful, gently-used items.

How will we know when we've been successful?

Picture in your minds what success will look like for you. Will it be when every child at the local homeless shelter receives his or her own stuffed animal? Or when a dozen new community-garden plots have been constructed in the local park? By defining your vision of success, you'll come up with specific measurements for charting your progress.

By the way, I think refrigerators are a marvelous place to store food. However, their true function, as we all know, is to serve as the family bulletin board. This is where you can put your checklist for what needs to be accomplished in order to reach your goals.

How much of my own time and money should I give to my child's project?

This all depends on who you are and what your resources are: The Kennedy family had the time and money to found The Special Olympics. Look at your resources. Do you have time? Money? Both?

Either way, you need to set out a reasonable budget—of both money and time. Your child will, of course, need to balance this responsibility with school, family obligations, after-school activities, play time, and other commitments. Likewise, your child needs to understand that you have a life, too, and that your family may not have the things that other families have. Susie's father, for example, had the freedom to use his office's copier to print the first edition of her newsletter. He could also drive her around to distribute them. But not every dad has access to a copier or a car.

Should I ask my child to give some of his or her own money towards the project?

Yes. Many children have a tremendous amount of discretionary spending money. One only has to look at MTV or Saturday-morning cartoons to realize how many ads are pitched towards children starting at a very young age. So tell your kids to put their money where their hearts are.

Many families ask their kids to give a portion of their allowance to charity each week, whether they're involved in a special volunteer project or not. (My friend Kathleen King insures that her son will donate some of his allowance each week to the church by giving it to him on Sunday mornings immediately before Mass.)

I personally believe, however, that you shouldn't ask your child to give a higher percentage of his or her money towards charity than you do. I'm pretty hard-nosed about this. It's not fair to demand that your kids donate 20% of their spending money to charity if you're not doing the same thing.

How can I make sure that neither I nor my child gets carried away with his or her charity project?

With kids, you have to be careful not to let them bite off more than they can chew. It's reasonable to commit to decorating 50 lunch bags a week for children at a shelter, so that the kids there can have a special treat at lunch. It's another thing for a nine-year-old to have the goal of single-handedly wiping out world hunger. Believe me, the lunch-bag goal is enough of a stretch as it is, and it is a very kind, charitable act of generosity and comfort.

Also, sometimes you may simply have to say no because what your child wants to do will take up too much family time or resources. In which case, you really need to compromise (a major part of raising children, and not one of the easier parts). Say your child wants to get involved in something that will take 20 hours per week of your time, and you have maybe two hours you can spare. You might need to stretch that to three hours, and ask your child to think a little smaller in order to make things work for both of you.

Where else can I find money and/or manpower to fuel this project?

If you don't have enough time or funds for your kid's project, it could prove an excellent opportunity to find other adults that might be able to lend a hand. In my opinion, godparents are grossly underutilized. To get them or other adults involved, your child should be the one who extends the invitation, and he or she needs to be clear about what their participation would entail. The trick to asking other adults is to make it clear to them that your child will accept a gracious "no" for an answer.

How can I involve our entire family?

One kid can't suck all the energy out of a family. If an older child is working on a pet charity project, figure out a supporting role that the younger kids can fulfill—besides just being annoying. Susie's younger sister, for example, wound up learning a lot about volunteering through her older sister, and took over Susie's work with the Miami Rescue Mission once Susie left for college.

Also, as Susie's grandmother and aunt prove, other relatives are often only too eager to help make your child's dream come true. Again, it needs to be your child, and not you, who asks for their help and outlines the specific ways they can contribute.

How should we celebrate once we reach our goal?

One of the challenges when doing charity work is that, with so much work to be done, many people don't take the time to stop and celebrate what they've accomplished.

I'm not talking about buying all the children involved an expensive gift. But some chocolate chip cookies and a juice-box toast can be a great way to commemorate reaching a goal. It's also a good time to ask each person involved to finish the sentences, "What I really liked about this project was..." and "If I had to do it all over again this is what I'd do differently." This can be a great, instructional way to both celebrate and process the experience.

How can I help my child sustain interest in this project over the long run?

Not all projects last forever. In fact, we don't necessarily want them to. We want there to be an end to AIDS and Alzheimer's and breast cancer.

Likewise, there needn't always be a "long run" for your child's dream. Just like a friendship or an interest in a sport or musical instrument, sometimes you have to let a volunteer project die a natural and graceful death.

For any undertaking you begin, you need to devise an exit strategy. Some projects, like making sandwiches for a soup kitchen, can be passed on to a sibling or to a more formal group, like a Girl or Boy Scout Troop. Or, simply tell those involved up front that the service your child is providing may not last forever.

You and your child might fall in love with the work and want to pursue it open-endedly, and there's nothing wrong with that. But one of the advantages of allowing yourselves some flexibility is that it gives your child a chance to explore different causes and projects. If you spend a year volunteering at an animal shelter, the next year you might want to raise funds for a mission trip for your church youth group. Your child will wind up with a very broad and impressive skills set— great for college or job applications, great for everyday life.

Mother-Daughter Days

The Big Question: How can volunteer work strengthen the bonds of family and friendship while teaching kids about charity at the same time?

When her older daughter Hilary was in grade school, Lynn Saperstein started a mother-daughter book club with five friends and their daughters to share their mutual love of reading and to create an opportunity for mother-daughter bonding. The group would meet once every other month to discuss a book they had all read independently—"quality books that were on the girls' level," as Lynn puts it—and sometimes the mothers would plan fun, educational outings that tied into the books' themes. When they read an Amelia Bedelia book in which the befuddled heroine visits a bank, Lynn arranged a trip to a local bank where the girls got a first-hand look at the inside of a safe. After they read an abridged version of *The Diary of Anne Frank,* they went to see the stage play of the same name.

But by the time the girls reached fifth or sixth grade, their increased homework loads left them little time or enthusiasm to read the chosen books. Soon, the mothers were coming to club meetings having done the reading, but the daughters hadn't.

This was not long before the girls would be making their bat mitzvahs, a rite of passage in the Jewish faith signifying the becoming of an adult member of society. (Girls make bat mitzvahs at age 12; boys make bar mitzvahs at age 13.) One of the key responsibilities of becoming an adult in the Jewish faith is philanthropy. So Lynn decided "it was the right time for them to start giving back to the community." She started over with a new agenda for the club. From here on out, the club would still count mothers and daughters as members. It would still meet once every two months, and mother-daughter bonding would still be a priority. But it would no longer be a book club. It would be a mitzvah club—"mitzvah" is a Hebrew word meaning "good deed"—and that's exactly what they would do: perform good deeds.

The Mitzvah Club's first mission was preparing meals at Project Open Hand, an AIDS organization. (Lynn had been close to a person who had died from the disease years before.) Lynn says that from that very first project, the girls were hooked on volunteerism, which she attributes partly to the fact that she had "handpicked these girls and their moms. I knew who would be into it—and more importantly, who would keep it a priority over the years."

As the girls got older, they and their moms walked and washed dogs at an animal shelter and went shopping for Operation Santa, which donates Christmas gifts to under-privileged kids. They helped disabled kids participating in track-and-field events as part of the Miracle League. They helped prepare meals for Meals on Wheels. They earned money by gift-wrapping books for donations at a Borders bookstore, then donated that money to an orphanage in Israel. They played bingo with the elderly at a nursing home. They passed out water to participants at the Atlanta Community Food Bank's Hunger Walk/Run.

Today, when Lynn recounts their varied volunteer projects, she can't help but laugh at the cherished memories, punctuating her sentences with declarations like "Oh, that was so much fun!" She explains: "It didn't have to be like we were curing the world. We just did little, fun, easy things—things I never got to do when I was a kid and some things I hadn't even done as an adult."

The mothers and daughters would take turns deciding what the group's next volunteer project would be, and each member would choose a cause that was close to her heart. One mother loved gardening, so for one mitzvah the girls potted small plants in pots they'd decorated by hand, then handed them out at a local nursing home. The mothers and daughters would, in theory, plan the activities as a team, but Lynn admits it was the parents who did most of the scheduling. "That's what a mom does: 'Hey kids, why don't we do this?' But the planning wasn't very hard, usually just a few phone calls." One thing the group did learn was to plan their activities well in advance; some local food banks had six-month waiting lists for volunteers!

Lynn says they always tried to give the girls opportunities to meet different types of people through their volunteer projects—and also give them the chance to talk about what they'd learned. Usually that just meant getting some ice cream after they were done volunteering to discuss what the girls liked about the project. Once, the club visited a homeless shelter where the girls played games with the kids there, while Lynn and her friends talked mom-to-mom with the women in the shelter. The girls were quite affected by that trip. "You could imagine bringing ten- and eleven-year-old girls to a homeless shelter, meeting people who don't have their own homes, kids who don't have any toys. Some of the girls were quite upset by those things. But we would always try to see where they were coming from and try to have them verbalize their feelings."

Eventually, Hilary and her friends went off to college. Lynn decided to start up a new Mitzvah Club with her younger daughter, Raleigh, and her friends. Raleigh thinks the Mitzvah Club has brought her closer to her mother—which had been the original point all along. "Being helpful always makes me happy," explains Raleigh, "and that happiness rubs off on the two of us when we're together."

How-To Questions

What age groups would most enjoy forming a charity club with their parents?

You can actually start a charity club at almost any age; four or five years old is really about the youngest. While teenagers might seem most suited for charity clubs, the challenge with them is all their other obligations, such as school, work, friends, sports, etc. If you start up the club before your kids reach high school and get caught up in other things, the chances of it staying together are much better.

How many parents and children should be involved?

Most groups find that five or six parents and five or six children are about the most a club can handle. More than that, and the kids (and/or parents) may form cliques within the club. Also, it can be a challenge to coordinate everybody's schedules and to find organizations that can accommodate a large number of volunteers at once.

How do we choose which of my child's friends to invite?

This is the same question all parents are forced to answer when they decide with whom they're going to carpool to school. (Carpools are the foxholes of suburbia.) You have to choose wisely. You may adore the parent but consider the kid a real monster, or vice versa. Look at the reliability of the parent and how he or she supervises the child. Does the parent pick up the child on time after a play date? Is the parent willing to give your kid a ride when you have an emergency? Does the child bite, kick or make other children cry? Does the parent yell at the child in front of other children?

Remember, the arrangement has to work for both you and your child. You may not particularly like one of your child's friends, but if they get along well, the parent is responsible, and the friend really isn't a bad influence, you may have to bite your tongue.

How often should we meet to volunteer?

Once a month is about all most families can handle— really, I'd recommend once every other month. Lynn Saperstein chose that time frame because she decided she'd rather meet less often but run the club successfully, instead of striving to meet more often and failing.

If you do decide to meet monthly, you might want to pick the first Saturday of every month rather than the last because of Halloween, Thanksgiving and Christmas, which all come at the end of the month. Or, you might decide that the club will go on hiatus during the holiday season, or over summer vacation, when families are pulled hither and yon with vacations, camps, and family reunions.

How should we choose our charity projects?

You might want to have just one person in charge of choosing the projects from month to month, if someone volunteers to take on that role. Along those lines, you can have each parent permanently in charge of a different part of the operation: one arranges transportation, another provides snacks, etc. Or rotate it every month, or put it to a vote every month, or choose one parent-child combo to be responsible for running the club for an entire year. There is no right method. You simply have to determine what is right for your group.

What kinds of volunteer opportunities work well for groups containing both adults and kids?

This will change through the years based on the physical, mental and emotional strengths and abilities of both the adults and the kids. Obviously, a group of six-year-olds can't fill sandbags when a flood is coming. On the flip side, a group of 15-year-olds might be bored with activities that appeal to younger kids. Make sure you don't choose a project that is going to test the very limits of human endurance, like building a house from scratch or damming up a river. But if you do have some hardy folks in your group, they might love to do something like constructing a garden for an inner-city park. Again, choosing projects shouldn't be a problem so long as everybody talks beforehand about what they like and dislike, what they want to learn more about, what talents they want to share, etc. There might be times here and there when a project doesn't agree with every member's sensibilities, but there's always next month's project.

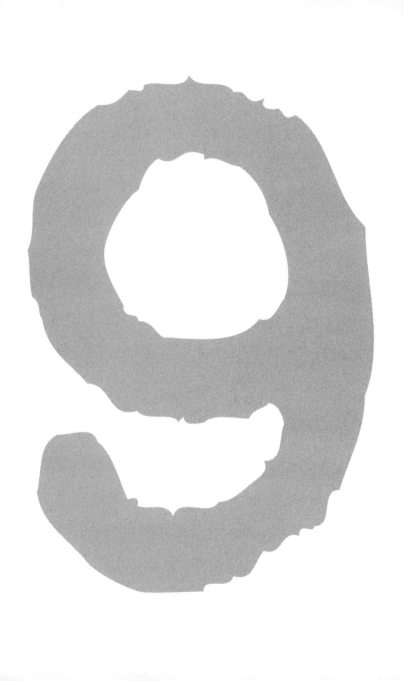

From Tragedy to Triumph

The Big Question: How can philanthropy and volunteering help my child cope with tragic world events?

The Bakewells are a busy, suburban family in St. Louis. Dad, Thomas, is an attorney and consultant. Mom, Julia, is a part-time marketing executive and veteran carpooler. Their children are nine-year-old Catherine and seven-year-old Myles. Like the rest of the world, the Bakewells sat in stunned silence in late December, 2004, watching the horrific images on the news as the Indian Ocean tsunami caused unimaginable devastation, killing more than one hundred thousand people and destroying the shores of entire countries.

The Bakewells talked about the disaster at home and at church. Catherine and Myles had trouble understanding how something this devastating could happen out of the blue. Catherine remembers being "really sad" about the tsunami. "I wasn't exactly crying, but I was kind of shocked when I watched the news. Then I saw the commercials about donating, and I thought I should do something."

In their quest for more information about the tsunami, Tom and Julia stumbled across an article about an orphanage in South Asia. Though nobody at the orphanage was prepared for a disaster of such magnitude, the children and staff, totaling about 40 people, had managed to scramble into the lone boat kept on hand in case of emergency. The orphanage sat directly in the path of the tsunami, yet not a single child was harmed during their escape.

Tom and Julia decided to share the story with their children, because they wanted them to hear something hopeful in the midst of so much destruction. Myles and Catherine were excited to hear that these children had survived.

About four weeks after the tsunami, Tom took a business trip to Bangkok to consult with the world relief organization Food for the Hungry. Tom's consulting engagement with the group was originally scheduled to take place in the U.S. Once the tsunami struck, the executives at Food for the Hungry had immediately traveled to South Asia so that they could best execute their relief efforts, and rescheduled Tom's work to take place in Thailand. (No wonder the group's slogan is, "We go to the hard places.")

Soon after Tom left, his kids e-mailed him in Bangkok. They decided they wanted to do something to help Food for the Hungry. Their father encouraged them from afar, writing, "It's important to help others however we can, whenever we can."

After brainstorming ways to raise money on her own, Catherine decided to market herself as a one-woman Hallmark store. She would start her own line of handmade greeting cards to raise money for the victims. She started going door to door taking orders for her wares and also took orders from members of her choir.

Younger brother Myles thought his sister was onto a good idea. He decided to sell handmade pictures door to door as well, but he would approach things a bit differently on the production end of his venture. He created his works of art beforehand, so that he could sell them on the spot. Entrepreneurially speaking, this made for a much more successful endeavor. Myles' customers got to see the goods up close, while Myles got the instant gratification of selling his handiwork. Catherine, meanwhile, had to go home and fill orders after she'd been out knocking on doors.

At first, Catherine was annoyed that her younger brother had copied her idea—and then all the more annoyed when Myles figured out how to do it more lucratively. Catherine also learned another life lesson the hard way when some of her choir friends, after pre-ordering cards from her, accepted them and then told her they didn't have any money.

But Catherine exhibited a remarkable amount of maturity when she chose to rise above the petty side of commerce. She decided that what mattered most was that both she and Myles were trying to help others. "At first I was mad that Myles was copying off of me, but he was doing it for the right reasons, so I wasn't mad for long. I felt proud of myself. My friend up the street even started to sell stuff, too." Catherine and Myles raised about $55 in total, which their mother sent to Food for the Hungry.

Julia called the principal of Myles' elementary school to tell him about her son's fundraising activities. Myles, who was in first grade, was recognized with an "On Eagle's Wings Award," an honor given to students who do something kind for another. Other kids at Myles' school latched onto the idea, and soon dozens of kids were making drawings and selling them to raise funds for tsunami relief.

According to Myles, "It would have been nice to use the money to buy a toy, but I was proud that I was doing the right thing. I donated the money not because I wanted to, but because it was the right thing. I'm glad the money went into the right hands."

Though Catherine and Myles both discovered how self-lessness is often the best feeling in the world, they're still kids. When their father finally returned from Bangkok, they rushed to fetch the box full of money they'd earned and proudly showed it to him. Then they asked, "Dad, what did you bring us?"

How-to Questions

When a tragic event takes place, what is the first thing I should do to help my child deal with it?

After you've all watched and absorbed the news footage, turn off the TV. Children can get very overwhelmed by sad or frightening messages with no plan for action.

Ask your child, "What do you think of that?" And then really listen to the answer. When something like the tsunami or Hurricane Katrina happens, children often think they're at risk, too. I know a five-year-old child in St. Louis who, after the tsunami, was very worried that the Mississippi River was going to swell up and drown everybody. Once he articulated this fear, his parents had the chance to explain why it wasn't, in fact, a reasonable concern.

After your child realizes that he or she isn't in any danger, explain the ways in which your family may already be helping. You might support certain organizations that help disaster victims, like Catholic Charities or the Red Cross. Or, your mosque or religious organization may have a branch in the affected region that is on the ground helping immediately.

This does two things. It reassures the child that if he or she were ever endangered or helpless in any way, help would be available. It also educates the child about where past gifts have gone, and how donations really do make a difference.

How do I help my child when he or she comes up with a plan to aid or raise money for others?

Start small and plan accordingly. Make sure your kid's project has a clear beginning, middle and end appropriate to his or her attention span. One of the reasons the Bakewells hold such good feelings about their work for Food for the Hungry is that the project didn't drag on, entail hours of work, or last forever.

A good way to keep things small is to think about parallel projects your kids can handle. For example, after 9/11, hearts around the world went out to the New York City firefighters who perished, as well as to the families they left behind. All across America, parents and kids talked about the firefighters in their own communities and the sacrifices they make—which provided an opportunity to bake some cookies and head down to the local firehouse to say, "Thank you for your willingness to keep us safe!"

Baking cookies and bringing them to the firehouse is a two-hour project at most. You don't need to form a non-profit corporation in order to give your children an outlet for channeling their thoughts and concerns. You don't have to raise a million dollars, and you don't have to get on Oprah. All it takes is one adult, one child, a little flour and some chocolate chips to teach a valuable lesson—and to help your child feel a little less powerless.

What steps can older kids take to help when tragedy strikes?

Older children (perhaps ages 10 and up) can be asked to research different charities and recommend where the family should donate. Unfortunately, in times of great catastrophe, scam artists look for great opportunities. Be sure to warn your child about the dangers of fake charities, especially when researching on the Internet. Have them make sure the charity is approved by the Better Business Bureau and that it's listed on Guidestar.org, a site that lists credible charities and non-profit organizations.

What if someone we know has been directly affected by the tragedy?

All charity doesn't have to take place through a volunteer organization or charity drive. It doesn't even have to take place between strangers. This is an opportunity for children to learn that, at times, we need to give time and money to family and friends as well. In many families, when one set of relatives may be financially helping another, the children aren't made aware of it. But children should be told when the family is going to help out, say, cousins in Pakistan whose home and school were destroyed by an earthquake. It lets children know that something, in fact, is being done to help these people.

In addition to showing kids how to financially give support, these events can teach kids how to give emotional support as well. This emotional support can come in many forms.

When the loss is personal—whether it's a house fire in the neighborhood or the death of an older relative from cancer—children can and should learn how to write a condolence letter. (I did say letter, not e-mail.) Your child can also help you make a tray of lasagna and deliver it to a neighbor who is going through a tough time.

As we mature and grow older, a lot of "volunteer work" really boils down to lending emotional support, offering an ear to listen and a shoulder to cry on. The best Meals on Wheels volunteers, after all, aren't the ones who can compete with Domino's for speedy delivery. They're the ones who bring a little kindness and warmth to a person as well as a hot meal. People who know how to do such things not only make for great volunteers—they also make for great people to be around.

Grumbling All the Way

The Big Question: How can I help my child get involved in giving when he or she isn't interested in the least—and I'm barely able to hold things together myself?

When Mary Alice married a handsome, wealthy European at age 19, little did she imagine what a mess she'd have on her hands by age 30. Ten years after their wedding, Mary Alice had separated from her husband, taking with her their two daughters, ten-year-old Mikki and seven-year-old Alex. Her dashing husband, Mary Alice had been horrified to discover, had been sexually abusing their older daughter. Mary Alice had stayed at home after the girls came along, so she had hardly any money of her own when she left. Her ex fled back to Europe, making it impossible for her to collect child support or press charges. Needless to say, times soon became tough for Mary Alice and her girls. Mary Alice was scared of being on her own, while her daughters were emotionally troubled and in need of attention.

As a newly-single parent, though, Mary Alice quickly adapted into the role of the straight-shooting pragmatist. She lucked into a job coordinating special events for a non-profit voluntary health agency. It offered low pay, but Mary Alice was excited to be a part of a family-friendly organization. She often had to work on weekends, running charity golf tournaments, walk-a-thons and other fundraising events. Babysitting was prohibitively expensive for Mary Alice, but that wasn't the only reason she chose to bring her daughters along with her on weekends. She wanted to spend time with them, and she wanted them to meet other adults who could be good role models.

The agency where Mary Alice worked was very sympathetic about her situation; in fact, many staff members and volunteers also brought their kids with them to weekend events. Mikki and Alex, however, weren't nearly as under-standing as Mary Alice's employers. Even though Mary Alice assigned her girls the easiest of tasks—making sure there were pencils in the golf carts, handing out bottled water to the walkers—they made it clear that they did not want to be there, doing more than their fair share of grousing and complaining. But Mary Alice, taking a hard tack, chose to simply ignore their protesting.

The "forced volunteering" didn't stop there. When Mikki was 16 years old, she was thrilled to receive a suspension for skipping school, thinking she'd get to stay home for a few days. Mary Alice, however, had different plans for her. She told her daughter, "You screwed up in school, so now it's time for you to do something for someone else"—namely, going into the office with her mother and working alongside her. Mikki remembers being so mad, she couldn't see straight. She pouted the entire day.

But even through her petulant haze, and despite her best efforts to act like a brat, Mikki was affected by the time she spent at her mother's office. She was touched by how kindly the other employees treated her, and she began to get a glimpse into her mother's work and the cause she dedicated herself to.

Slowly, Mikki's attitude about volunteerism started to change for the better. For one thing, she grew into a teenage girl who actually wanted to volunteer at the walk-a-thons that were held on college campuses, because it gave her the opportunity to meet cute older guys—which may not be the most selfless way to get interested in charity, but at least it was effective. More significantly, though, Mikki started to see how she could really make a difference in other people's lives. She started to understand her mother's ethics regarding charity: If you have a minute, you give a minute. If you have a dollar, you give a dollar.

Around the age of 18, Mikki started to branch out and take the initiative in her volunteer work. She decided—entirely on her own—to volunteer for a victim services group. As a former victim of child abuse, she wanted to offer support to younger girls who had endured what she had endured. Once a week, Mikki and a therapist met with a group of a dozen girls to talk about their problems. But the commitment proved to be too much for Mikki to handle. Looking back, she now says, "The girls and I really connected, but it was a really hard thing for me to do. Every time I saw these girls, I went through my own pain all over again. I was too young to be doing that kind of volunteer work. It just hurt too much. I embraced the work, but it was the wrong place at the wrong age."

Mary Alice was supportive of Mikki's search for the right volunteer opportunity, telling her to hang in there and to keep looking for a well-suited position. Eventually, Mikki found a mentoring program that allowed her to spend time with kids—helping them with their homework, or sometimes just sitting and talking with them. Mikki found this experience totally rewarding. "There was one 12-year-old girl named Jessica who would just light up when I came in the door," she says. "All the kids at this program were from broken homes, and I was happy to serve as a mentor for them, since my parents were divorced as well."

Younger sister Alex didn't need quite as much prodding and punishment to become an enthusiastic volunteer. She loved getting to meet some of the celebrities who made appearances at her mother's charity events, including famous hockey players and soap opera stars. Getting to bring along a friend also helped make it fun, and so did getting to see her mother in another role. But she also loved, as she explains it today, "feeling very involved and alive and that I had a purpose. When you are from a broken home, you wonder where you belong in life. What is your purpose? Volunteering was a wonderful form of instant gratification for me. At the end of the day, I felt important and great and swollen with pride. It was often the only time in the week I felt really good about myself—which was probably what my mom was hoping for all along."

Alex, now a 33-year-old single mother of two, still had to weather her share of hard knocks in life. She got pregnant while she was in high school, delivering her first child two months after she graduated. But she still makes time today to volunteer. On the Fourth of July, Alex traditionally organizes a Good Neighbor Day for her community. She works in the insurance industry, but she's still looking for the perfect job in the non-profit sector where she can work with kids and put to use the college degree she earned in elementary education. Says Alex, "I want to lead something really big with a purpose. But if I don't land that dream job, there will always be volunteering. It gives me a sense of purpose and pride."

Mikki, now, is a 36-year-old mother with a five-year-old daughter of her own—and also carves out time in her busy schedule for volunteering. Says Mikki, "Volunteering gives me inner peace. Even if it's only for an hour, I am able to put a smile on somebody's face. I'm so glad my mother didn't listen to my complaining and made me keep going. I'm hooked for life."

How-to Questions

How can I make my children volunteer if they don't want to?

We parents have to make our children do a lot of things they don't want to do: eat their vegetables, get their shots, and yes, even volunteer from time to time. The goal, of course, is that eventually they'll grow up to like veggies and volunteering—although shots may never be a favorite. All these "have-tos" are part of our parental responsibility to keep them safe and well-fed, as well as to help them form a solid value system.

This being said, one of the keys to introducing reluctant children to volunteerism and philanthropy is to give them some control over the situation. The more choices you can give them—within reason—the better. For instance, when I used to take my sons to the doctor, I'd ask them, "Would you like to have the shot in the right arm or the left arm?"

The choice was never whether or not to get the shot; that was non-negotiable.

You may want to ask your child, "Would you rather volunteer with your friend Ralphie or take your friend Max?" Or you may want to let your child pick out the snacks to bring along for an afternoon of volunteering.

What do I do if my child is at an age when he or she might create a scene?

There are places where kids who might exhibit bad behavior shouldn't be allowed. If, for instance, your child has been having temper tantrums lately, then a senior center or hospital ward is not a great place for him or her to volunteer. But an outdoor project that involves wide, open spaces, heavy lifting, and a lot of adult supervision might actually be a wonderful way for an overenergetic kid to focus all that energy into something positive.

Just as there's no such thing as a truly bad kid, there are no truly bad volunteer projects. There are only those projects that might not be suitable for your child's age or temperment. You'll probably have to work a little harder to find a good match for your potential problem child, but once you do find a good one, it might end up being the X-factor that turns the kid's attitude around.

What if I can't be there to help chaperone my problem child at a volunteer site?

Volunteering is not to be confused with therapy or babysitting. Even when you're not around, it's still your job to make sure your child is safe and comfortable, and that he or she won't be a menace to others. If you're not going to be at the volunteer site, share information about your child with the head chaperone. Explain if there's a recent personal loss that might affect your child's behavior, or if there are any special medical issues to take into account, like an inhaler for asthma. Always make sure the supervisor can contact you immediately by phone in case of an emergency.

What if my child really can't stand the project?

Sometimes, as with Mikki, there is a bad fit. In her case, working with a victim services group wasn't right for her—even though she had the best of intentions—because she was too young to deal with the deep-seeded problems of the girls she was counseling.

Other times, kids have expectations that are out of line with their skills; they may have their heart set on building a new house with Habitat for Humanity, and don't want to hear that they're too young to take on such a construction project all by themselves.

Sometimes it's simply a matter of cliques, just like in any school situation where your kid might be the odd one out.

As a parent, it's your job to assess the situation, see how long the commitment will take, decide whether you should intervene, and then decide whether a new project should be found.

Remember, having a sulky, miserable kid around is unpleasant for everybody involved in the project.

If all else fails, you can always ask your child to take on extra chores at home for extra money, then help him or her donate that money (or at least a portion of it) to a charity of his or her choosing. As they say, sometimes discretion is the better part of valor.

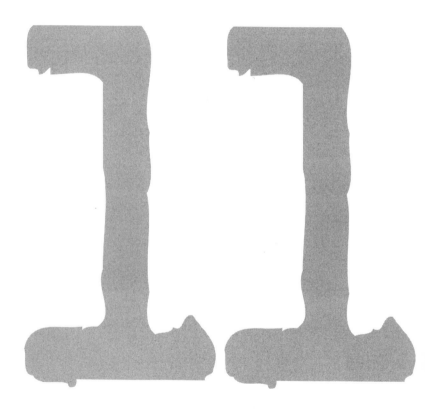

Conclusion
They're Always Watching

When recalling childhood memories, how often do you later find out that things weren't as you remembered them at all?

My husband and I were once visiting my husband's brother, John, and his wife, Jill. We were talking about Frank and John's grandparents. John said, "My grandfather was the head veterinarian at the Bronx Zoo. He caught a disease from one of the apes and died. My grandmother was so devastated, she died six months later from a broken heart."

I piped in, "Your grandmother died six months later of tuberculosis in a sanitarium in upstate New York." John insisted that I was wrong and that his grandmother had, in fact, died of a broken heart. I, however, had heard the story as an adult from his mother and felt pretty confident in my source.

It doesn't really matter, fifty years later, whether John's grandmother died of TB, a broken heart, or a little of both. The reason I tell this story is to illustrate how children observe and remember things differently—which is why we need to take the time to explain our actions to them.

Whether we're conscious of it or not, we all have a philosophy of giving. Do you give money to panhandlers on the street? Always, never, sometimes? Gloria Steinem, the great feminist activist, has said that she always gives money to homeless women on the street. Her mother had schizophrenia, and she believes that, had circumstances been different, her mother could have very easily wound up on the street like them.

My older son, Teddy, always gives money to Hare Krishnas when he passes them on the street. When he was backpacking through Europe a few years ago, he was without funds for a couple days while waiting for a check to clear. The Hare Krishnas in Amsterdam fed him a meal while he was down and out—something he will never forget.

I have a client who belongs to Alcoholics Anonymous; he never gives to the homeless. He believes that doing so is just enabling the drunks to get drunker. He does, however, donate directly to homeless shelters.

Let's say you are the type of person who does not believe in giving money to people on the street. You probably have a very good reason why you choose not to. But when you're out with your child and he or she sees you walking past a homeless person without stopping to help, all your child sees is that you just ignored a person in need.

This is what I call a "teachable moment," and in order to make it into a learning opportunity, the first thing that you should do is stop. Take a few minutes and find a place to sit down. Get a cup of hot chocolate with your child if you can, and say to him or her, "I always/never/sometimes give to people on the street because..." Explain your philosophy. And remind your child that someday he or she will have the opportunity to develop his or her own philosophy of giving.

You may also want to talk to your child about workplace giving, to which a child is rarely privy. When we use payroll deduction at work to give to the United Way or the Combined Health Appeal or the Women's Fund—and even when we write out checks to these and other groups while paying the bills at home—our children have no idea that we are involved in supporting our community. But they will take notice when there is a charity telethon on TV and Mom and Dad aren't calling in to make pledges. Again, take time to explain when and how you give, and why you choose to give to certain charities over others.

As I've said throughout this book, giving money is terrific, but the gift of time is equally important. After my kids' former babysitter, Liz, retired, I used to have lunch with her once a year. One year, after Liz's husband went into a nursing home, the next-door neighbor began mowing her lawn for her. She tried time and again to pay him, but he absolutely refused. Liz's husband, Johnny, had always lent this neighbor tools and helped him out whenever he needed it.

One day Liz looked out the window and saw her neighbor's son mowing her lawn. She went outside and asked, "Where is your dad?" The son replied, "He had a heart attack. He's in the hospital, but I think he's going to be OK." Liz said, "Wait right here, I want to pay you." The 14-year-old replied, "I'm sorry, ma'am, but I can't take your money. That's not how we do things."

Liz was floored by this boy's honorable stance. She put on her hat, went to the store, and picked up the ingredients to make his family a huge plate of fried chicken. Despite the father's cardiac problems, this family obviously had a good heart. (However, Liz should probably lay off the fried foods as gifts, just in case the neighbor's son inherited his dad's bad cholesterol along with his good heart!)

This young man had taken over where his father had left off. This young man, who had seen his father voluntarily mow his elderly neighbor's lawn, knew that following in his father's footsteps was the right thing to do. What more could a parent ask?

Resources

The following is just a small sampling of the thousands of reputable charities and organizations out there that would love to receive donations of your time and money. They represent an infinite cross-section of worthy causes: the environment, poverty, the elderly, literacy, cancer, the arts, disaster relief, homelessness, endangered species, etc.

Some of them serve as information clearinghouses about child-friendly philanthropy; most offer volunteer opportunities for philanthropists both young and old.

In addition to perusing this list (categorized alphabetically by the organizations' names) visit our website, www.raisingcharitablechildren.com, to check out updated lists of recommended charities and charitable resources, to share your own great stories and resources, and to sign up for our free newsletter.

1-800-Volunteer.org
http://www.1-800-volunteer.org
Sponsored by the Points of Light Foundation (and also affiliated with familycares.org or kidscare.org), this Web site connects families to local volunteer centers in their communities and gives adults ideas for teaching kids about philanthrophy.

Alzheimer's Association
www.alz.org
More than 35,000 volunteers work toward an end to Alzheimer's and optimize the quality of life for those affected by

the disease. Numerous volunteer opportunities are available, even for those who can spare only a couple hours per week.

American Cancer Society

www.cancer.org

The American Cancer Society offers numerous charity events and volunteer opportunities for those who want to help fight the battle against cancer.

American Heart Association

www.americanheart.org

Those who sign up online to become members of the AHA's Grassroots Network receive newsletters with information on how to call, write or visit elected officials at the federal and state levels to express their views on important health issues. Fun, kid-friendly fundraising opportunities are also available

American Hiking Society

www.americanhiking.org/events/vv

The American Hiking Society offers about 100 volunteer-vacation opportunities per year, giving participants a chance to help renovate or maintain campsites and public lands. Vacations usually last six or seven days and cost $130 for newcomers, which includes a year's membership and is usually tax-deductible.

Center for a New American Dream

www.newdream.org

This non-profit group's mission is to help Americans discover innovative ways to help the environment, stand up for social justice, and become more conscious consumers. It accepts monetary donations and volunteers on its own behalf, but it also directs people towards charities with similar visions. New American Dream also co-founded (with the World Wildlife Fund) a youth-oriented campaign called Be, Live, Buy Different—Make A Difference.

Cross-Cultural Solutions

www.crossculturalsolutions.org

This international organization operates vacation-like volunteer programs, many of them suitable for families, in foreign countries such as Brazil, China, Costa Rica, Russia, and Thailand.

Do Something

www.dosomething.org

Do Something offers fun projects and programs in community building, health and the environment that help kids develop life skills and give them the chance to lead. The organization also offers philanthropy curricula to schools and challenges kids to find ways to help out in their communities.

Energize Inc.

www.energizeinc.com

A source of information for those involved in volunteer management, Energize offers articles on non-profit know-how (like volunteer recruitment and preventing fundraising burnout). A referral network on the site helps users find conferences, workshops, reading materials and other educational aids geared towards strengthening volunteer involvement.

Give.org

www.give.org

A clearinghouse of information on making monetary and material donations to charity, Give.org also offers tips on "wise giving" and issues reports on charitable organizations.

Global Literacy Project

www.glpinc.org

The GLP's mission is to create libraries, multimedia centers and literacy support groups in rural or distressed communities throughout the world. Schools, businesses and groups can sort and pack book donations and work on specific efforts in Africa, the Caribbean or Latin America; volunteers in the New Jersey area are most needed, as that is where GLP is based.

Global Volunteers

www.globalvolunteers.org

Since 1984, Global Volunteers has placed individuals, groups and families in suitable community-service vacations around the country and the globe: literacy programs in the Cook Islands, construction projects in the Mississippi Delta, peace-advancing workshops in Northern Ireland. Volunteer coordinators can help you find the right volunteer vacation and accommodations.

Green Volunteers

www.greenvolunterrs.org

An information network all about nature conservation efforts and how to help them, this website lists some 500 environmental projects worldwide in need of volunteers: short-term and long-term commitments, water or land-based conservation.

Idealist.org

www.idealist.org

This Web site, maintained by the activist group Actions Without Borders, lists more than 50,000 nonprofit and community organizations around the world. The site lets users search and choose their perfect volunteer opportunities among the thousands available.

International Book Project

www.intlbookproject.org

Since 1966, the International Book Project has been promoting literacy and cross-cultural understanding around the world by organizing shipments of books and other reading materials to the needy. IBP encourages individuals and groups interested in helping them to donate money, sponsor book shipments, or get involved in back-to-school book exchange programs.

JustGive.org

www.justgive.org

Just Give's mission is to connect people with charities and causes they want to help financially. Users can search or browse through more than 1,000,000 charities, purchase charity gift certificates or create online charity registries for weddings or other special occasions.

Little Brothers—Friends of the Elderly

www.littlebrothers.org

With nine urban locations across the country, Little Brothers aims to not only provide needed services to the elderly, but also to help them build new friendships and celebrate life.

MuseumStuff

www.museumstuff.com

This international database lists thousands of museums by state, artists and educational topics.

Natural Resources Defense Council

www.nrdc.org

One of the largest and most influential environmental-protection groups, the NRDC maintains an on-line Earth Axtivist Network that provides information on ways to help with specific environmental issues (including letter-writing campaigns) as well as the Green Squad, a kid-friendly activist network that encourages children to campaign for environmentally safer, green-friendly schools.

NetAid

www.netaid.org

NetAid raises awareness and promotes action among the world's wealthy countries (including the U.S.) by offering educational programs on poverty for children and adults alike, spreading the word about poverty, and connecting volunteers with suitable projects. Special youth programs include the Global Citizen Corps and the Global Action Awards.

Network for Good

www.networkforgood.org

This nonprofit organization uses the Web to help individuals and families become more involved in their communities through volunteering and donating. Its Youth Volunteer Network motivates kids to take action.

Points of Light Foundation

www.pointsoflight.org

This national network of volunteer centers promotes youth and family volunteering across America through such initiatives as the International Youth Hall of Fame and Youth Engaged in Services Ambassadors.

Rebuilding Together

www.rebuildingtogether.org

"Helping homeowners live in safety, warmth and independence" is the slogan for this organization, which provides free home repairs and revitalizations to low-income homeowners. Most local affiliates of Rebuilding Together accept teenage volunteers. In addition to year-round programming, Rebuilding Together sponsors a National Rebuilding Day, usually on the last Saturday in April.

Sierra Club

www.sierraclub.org

Open to members and nonmembers alike, Sierra Club's national service trips can take you anywhere from Alaska to Hawaii, Puerto Rico to the Virgin Islands. Prices may range from $300 to $1,000 per person.

The Third Wave Foundation

www.thirdwavefoundation.org

Third Wave aims to empower young women and and helps them learn how to become social activists. Through grants and scholarships, Third Wave gives direct financial support to young women activists and the organizations they lead.

VolunteerAmerica

www.volunteeramerica.net

VolunteerAmerica connects individuals, families and groups with volunteer opportunities and vacations on public lands all across America, such as hiking trails and national parks.

VolunteerMatch

www.volunteermatch.org

This online service helps people get involved with community-service organizations throughout the United States. The site can connect volunteers to one of 38,000 service organizations and 36,000 specific volunteer jobs.

Wilderness Volunteers
www.wildernessvolunteers.org
Since 1997, Wilderness Volunteers has coordinated efforts with the National Park Service, the Forest Service, the Bureau of Land Management and the U.S. Fish and Wildlife Service to create volunteer vacations that improve public lands.

World Hunger Year
www.worldhungeryear.org
World Hunger Year attacks poverty and hunger at the root of the problem, promoting community-based solutions that lead to short-term relief and long-term self-reliance. WHY's "Get Active Center" shows you how to get involved in numerous ways: planning a fundraising event in your community, spreading the word on topical issues, lobbying your elected officials, or finding local volunteer opportunities via its National Hunger Clearinghouse (which can also be accessed by calling 800-GLEAN-IT). There are also specific guidelines for involving children in such projects.

Youth On Board
www.youthonboard.org
Youth On Board prepares young people to become leaders in their communities through customized workshops and technical assistance. Since 1994, Youth On Board has trained more than 12,000 young people and worked with 380 schools and organizations.

Acknowledgements

I want to start with my grandmother, whom I never met. She was a very wealthy woman in Hanover, Germany, who held weekly gatherings for local artists in her enormous drawing room (so big, it held two Bechstein concert grand pianos). According to my mother, when the artists would thank their hostess and get ready to leave, the housekeeper would usher them to the front door, then tell them to sneak around to the back of the house by the kitchen. There, she would give them huge baskets of food to see them through the week. The artists were meant to think that my grandmother was clueless about this little ritual. Of course, she had engineered the whole thing.

I want to thank my father's family who, unlike my mother's family, was very poor. They sacrificed and worked to put my father through medical school. He, in turn, put a cousin of mine through medical school. It is now my generation's turn to pony up for school, camp and the like, which we do when it is needed.

I am always inspired by my stable of guinea pigs—I mean, children. My son Teddy (known in New York, where he lives, as Frank Robbins) is an actor and a cycling advocate. His favorite charity is Transportation Alternatives. His wife, Laura, brought a new dimension to our family's Joy and Sadness meetings by suggesting that we commit more volunteering time to those charities we like but don't have enough funds to commit to financially. Laura's favorite charity is the Children's Home Society of Virginia.

My second son, Jono Robbins, is a high school ceramics teacher in St. Louis. His favorite charities are McClure North High School, where he happens to teach, and the Animal Protective Association of Granite City, Illinois, from which he adopted his beloved dog, Milo. Our niece, age 17 and also named Carol Weisman, has lived with my husband and me for six years. Her list of favorite charities includes the four choirs in which she sings and the Anytown Youth Leadership Institute, run by the longest acronym ever, NCCJSTL (which stands for National Conference for Community and Justice of Metropolitan St. Louis).

One of my favorite charities has always been The Learning Disabilities Association—which brings me to my list of helpful experts who make it all, including this book, possible.

First and foremost is the lovely and talented Rose Martelli. She writes, she edits. She does research and if I had another daughter, I would want her to be just like Rose. Rose is a sucker for a non-profit direct mailer and gives regularly to Planned Parenthood, the National Organization for Women, and just about any group or politician affiliated with the word "Democrat."

Next is the famous "Webgranny," Nanka, who makes all things technical work around here. She is an avid environmentalist who is active in Heifer International.

On a good day, I look like the middle-aged love child of Henry Kissinger and Barbra Streisand. But my photographer, Suzy Gorman—who is partial to the Jackie Joyner-Kersee Boys and Girls Club—always makes me look terrific. Not so terrific, though, that my clients can't recognize me in an airport! She is truly gifted.

When I told the amazing artist Yvo Riezebos to design a book cover for me that was "Mr. Rogers meets Bette Midler," he totally got it. His favorite charity is Hope House, a shelter for battered and abused women in Kansas City, Missouri.

Most of all, I want to thank my sweet husband, Frank Robbins. I fell in love with Frank when he said, "Jane Fonda might be attractive if she weren't so skinny." Heaven!

After all these years, the highlight of my day is still the moment when Frank walks into the house. His favorite charities are the Alliance Francaise and little ol' moi. When I wanted to invite my niece to live with us, he said, "Of course." With every gift of time and money I make, he is totally supportive. I can't think of anyone else with whom I'd rather have raised our children.

SOME OF CAROL'S MOST REQUESTED KEYNOTES AND WORKSHOPS:

For Associations, Clubs, and Nonprofits:

Raising Charitable Children: Creating Generations of Friends

Raising Charitable Children: Your Leadership Legacy

Raising Charitable Children (Even When You are Occasionally Short on Funds, Time or Just Feel a Little Crabby)

For Independent Schools, Colleges, Universities and Other Alumni Groups:

Raising Charitable Children: A Major Donor Workshop: Carrying on the Tradition of Caring. (Also applicable to nonprofit groups)

The Janus Approach to Fundraising: Facing the Future, Appreciating the Past

The Joy and Power of Giving Together, From Alumni Giving Circles to Family Foundations

For Financial Institutions, Insurance Companies, Corporate Employers and Others:

The Joys of Raising Charitable Children

The Giving Family

Giving More than Money: Transferring Values from Generation to Generation

To schedule Carol, call her at **314-863-4422** in the United States or e-mail her at **Carol@BoardBuilders.com**

OTHER BOOKS BY CAROL...

Secrets of Successful Boards:
The Best from the Nonprofit Pros
F.E. Robbins & Sons Press, 1998, 2001, 2006

Secrets of Successful Retreats:
The Best from the Nonprofit Pros
F.E. Robbins & Sons Press, January, 2003

Secrets of Successful Fundraising:
The Best from the Nonprofit Pros
F.E. Robbins & Sons Press, 2000

Build a Better Board in 30 Days:
A Practical Guide for Busy Trustees
F.E. Robbins & Sons Press, 1998

Losing Your Executive Director
without Losing Your Way
Carol Weisman, Richard I. Goldbaum
Jossey-Bass, 2004

The Business Professional's
Guide to Nonprofit Board Service
Charles F. Dambach, Oliver Tessier, Carol E. Weisman
BoardSource, 2002

A Corporate Employee's Guide to
Nonprofit Board Service
National Center for Nonprofit Boards, June, 1996

If you have an idea or resource for

Raising Charitable Children

that you'd like to share,

if you would like to order
additional copies of this book,

if you would like to
purchase Carol's other books,

if you would like Carol to facilitate
your family foundation meeting,

or

if you would like to
schedule Carol as a speaker,
you can reach us at

www.RaisingCharitableChildren.com

or

314-863-4422

We'd love to hear from you!